LUCIEN AND I

A Collage Novel

LUCIEN AND I

A Collage Novel

Danny Wynn

Bright Lights Big City Publishing

Regarding material quoted herein, please see the
Acknowledgments section.

Editor: Lorraine Fico-White
www.magnificomanuscripts.com

Co-editor: Julie Mosow
Cover Painting: Nancy Zarider

Lucien and I
Danny Wynn

1. Title   2. Author   3. Fiction

LCCN: 2015903692
ISBN: 978-0-692-39964-4

For Toby and Billie

"Now, at twenty-four, he has come to a time of choice. I know quite well how all that is. And then, I read his letters. His father writes to him in the most beautiful, educated hand, the born hand of a copyist, admonitions to confront life, to think a little more seriously about this or that. I could have laughed. Words that meant nothing to him. He has already set out on a dazzling voyage which is more like an illness, becoming ever more distant, more legendary. His life will be filled with those daring impulses which cause him to disappear and next be heard of in Dublin, in Veracruz… I am not telling the truth about Dean, I am creating him out of my own inadequacies, you must always remember that."

James Salter
A Sport and a Pastime

CHAPTER 1

Late August 1994.

It was around three in the morning in a pulsating Istanbul nightclub when I caught Lucien's eye. The club was called Twenty-Nineteen—written *2019*—and we were dancing with the exquisite Azine, Lucien's Turkish ex-girlfriend who lived in the Eurasian city—light brown hair, golden skin, stylish, the epitome of feminine elegance as far as I could see. We were moving loosely, sweat-drenched, Lucien in that whirling, psychedelic dervish way of his. I was in a transcendent state, one of those all-too-rare moments when the pure act of dancing makes you high, fills you with euphoria. I caught his eye and shouted above the blasting techno-soul, "I'm alive!"

He nodded and grinned his grin. He knew.

That's the way he made me feel. He enhanced my capacity to enjoy life, made the good times better. And the most acute thread of the feeling was the sensation of living life to the full, which I yearned for like a parched plant with long twisting roots seeking moisture. The sensation was a drug for me, just a notch or two below the jolt of ego-juice a guy gets when a sexy woman looks at him with desire, or better yet, succumbs. Some of my many demons.

I was a creature in search of exaltation.

There was, however, an element of desperation in my quest, and in the moments, or longer times, when I was in the sought-after state, the heady pleasure was bolstered by a strong sense of relief at having made it to that elusive place.

In a way, the trip to Istanbul was the peak of my friendship with Lucien and the night at *2019* the high point of the expedition. Not in any exact sense. It's just that when I look back, Istanbul seems like the pinnacle of our bond, and the night at the club the time we soared the highest. The experience of connecting, of shared good times, was distilled to its very essence. And yet the stain was already there, dark and spreading.

In the course of that night and the thirty-six hours leading up to it, I experienced a powerful transporting effect. The day before, I'd been at work in midtown Manhattan, sitting at my desk in my twenty-sixth floor corner office, staring south out the floor-to-ceiling window at the Sixth Avenue canyon, living my stultified conventional life. My assistant buzzed me to say the car service was waiting downstairs. I grabbed my black canvas travel bag off the black leather couch and headed to JFK. Flew direct to Istanbul overnight to join Lucien. He'd already been in Europe for almost a month and then in Turkey for a week where he'd been traveling with Azine and Giles. Azine had lived in New York a couple of years back, which was when they'd been romantically involved. Giles was an old friend of his from their days at a posh public school in some rural English town. I hadn't met either of them, and I don't mix overly well with a lot of people, but I was optimistic. After all, it was Lucien.

On arrival, I picked up a rental car and drove north along the western shore of the Bosporus in the blindingly bright morning light, listening to an advance copy of the new *Jesus and Mary Chain* album. Somebody at work had handed it to me as I left, with a shout of endorsement. I was headed to Bebek, a former fishing village swallowed up by the sprawling metropolis, now a fashionable neighborhood in the northern part of the city, on the European side of the enormous strait.

"Allo, Chas," Lucien said in his mock-Cockney accent. He drew out the phrase as much as possible with only three syllables as he strolled up to my outdoor table at the Bebek Café smoking a cigarette. I'd called him at

Azine's apartment across the way from my hotel, and he'd told me to meet him at the café. By the way, my name's not Chas, but it was a snippet of dialogue from a movie that Lucien liked to wrap his mouth around at the time.

I was drinking a thick dark Turkish coffee. The clack of backgammon pieces and rustle of dice came from tables around me. The Muslim call to prayer wafted over from outdoor speakers on top of a tall pole outside the small mosque across the alley. A smile came to my face, as it usually did when I saw Lucien's rascally visage.

"Natasha?" he asked with a grin. He'd had told me to ask for Azine's friend, Natasha, when I checked into my hotel.

"Oh, yeah," I said. "I forgot. Jet lag and all."

"That's a shame. Natasha is Turkish slang for all the Russian prostitutes flooding the city these days. I was wondering how they were going to react at the front desk."

That first night was when Azine took us up in the hills above the Bosporus to *2019*. The club was in an abandoned auto junkyard on a sloping hillside, shrubbery here and there and empty oil drums scattered around with fires blazing inside. At the top of the hill, a spotlight shone on an ancient, crumbling ruin. The scene was Mad Max goes to Istanbul. Apocalyptic Constantinople.

On the far side of the shadowy junkyard was a sprawling multi-level structure built into the hillside, pulsing with crunching rhythms. We walked up a long ramp to the entrance, though, as I soon saw, the distinction between inside and outside was blurred. There was a long sidewall made of scaffolding partly covered by canvas, containing elevated walkways crowded with people overlooking the dancers inside.

To the right after entering, backed up against the hillside, was a high wall formed by an enormous concrete slab with girder-like pieces of rusty steel sticking out at skewed angles—an enormous modern sculpture of sorts. At the other end of the space was a swarming dance floor, partly open to the night sky, flanked by two hulking brick furnaces with huge smokestacks rising above. At the top of them were large gothic-style openings with dancers writhing inside, lit up by flickering lights as if in flames. You get the idea.

Shortly after we arrived, Lucien disappeared briefly with Azine and returned with a grin, saying, "Let's bang on an E!"

Quickly and smoothly, with the help of the rhythms and the drug, we became caught up in a trance-like bacchanalia. The powerful transporting effect was then completed for me—from my lofty pressure-filled office in Manhattan to the decadent pumping night in the hills of Istanbul. A jolting rejuvenating sea change. Exhilarating, cleansing.

That was when I caught Lucien's eye across the dance floor and shouted, "I'm alive!"

We stayed at *2019* until six in the morning. I couldn't have done it without the ecstasy. On top of everything else, my body clock was completely out of whack. As the darkness gave way to pale light, Giles and I were standing outside in the auto junkyard leaning against a gigantic tire on its side, about a dozen feet in diameter and half as wide. I couldn't imagine what kind of vehicle used a tire that size. I was limp. I had moved past the transporting effect into disorientation. Azine came down the ramp and announced we were going to somebody's house in the countryside. The bed in my hotel room beckoned, oh, so sweetly. But hey, I was on a journey and didn't resist with any real conviction.

We joined a small caravan of other cars and as the sun began to rise drove out of the city into a landscape that looked like the surface of the moon. Barren and arid, hard-baked, rocky. At two points along the highway, both in the middle of nowhere, a vast unfinished building complex loomed, set back from the road, seemingly abandoned mid-construction, adding distinctly to the wasteland effect. In the other cars apparently were some Turkish club promoters and their entourage, and the DJ of the night imported from Amsterdam, along with his crew, which turned out to include two exceptionally beautiful Dutch women and a scraggly Australian guy whose "thing" was drawing temporary tattoos.

After almost an hour, we arrived at an isolated stone

farmhouse on a rise above the surrounding plain. The house was white except for the terracotta roof and looked well-maintained, with oasis-like landscaping and a shimmering-white swimming pool in the back. My state of being had begun to enter the surreal. As our motley crowd milled around on the front terrace, our Turkish host went inside and came out a few minutes later with a woman who seemed to be the housekeeper and who'd clearly just been woken up. He barked at her in Turkish, and she went back inside. To make coffee, he announced. The group settled down at a large wooden table and in nearby outdoor armchairs under a vine-covered trellis. Everybody seemed to be in a daze. It still wasn't much past sunrise.

Our host was a young Turkish guy dressed Versace-style, with short dark hair cut crisply and lightly oiled. He was effeminate, though there was a young woman in the group who seemed to be romantically attached to him. She had lovely plump breasts under a tight black T-shirt with the word *Chanel* stretched over them in white lettering. The guy flitted about and seemed quite pleased with his impromptu gathering.

The housekeeper emerged with a large tray of coffee, orange juice and sliced baguettes, and set it down on the table. Our host berated her in Turkish and seemed to issue more orders. After she left, he said something about her being a drug addict. I could only imagine what the background to their arrangement might be.

I wasn't particularly bothered by the Turk's treatment of the housekeeper, but Giles took extreme offense. Off to the side where the others couldn't hear, he muttered to Lucien and me, "The guy is being a complete asshole to the poor woman, roused out of bed at dawn to wait on a bunch of club-addled strangers. And he's doing it just to impress us."

It sounded like he might be right, but we were guests in a remote foreign place and my condition didn't allow for much of a reaction to anything. Lucien, however, said to Giles, "Yeah, you're right. The guy's a complete wanker. You ought to slap him around a bit."

Giles' appearance belied him. Tall and thin, with an eye-catching mane of long curly blond hair and refined facial features, he seemed at first glance almost feminine, not physically imposing. And yet he was an ex-aristobrat, still with a taste for a bit of wild-boy behavior. He strongly subscribed to the school of thinking-man's vulgarity that Lucien and I embraced. He might even have been a step or two beyond us in that regard. He was engaging, sometimes in a nasty funny way. I was enjoying his company.

His dislike of our host went beyond the treatment of the servant. The guy just rubbed Giles the wrong way. I had to admit the Turk was a prime candidate for the *Coffee Table Book*. Lucien and I had a running joke about creating a coffee table book of social slugs, the unctuous sycophants who hang around the periphery of glamorous social scenes, perversely embracing and reinforcing the very values that keep them on the outskirts. We already had several candidates, among them Doug the Slug, Peggy aka "Piggy" (a pushy PR woman who wore outfits intended for women fifty or sixty pounds lighter), and The Original Slug (an exceptionally grotesque guy we ran across often in the overlapping downtown New York scenes, who was obsessed with hanging out with hip beautiful people and drove a party van from event to event with like-minded pals). Our plan was to get the subjects to pose elaborately, maybe tell them the theme of the book was hip offbeat people, and shoot the photos in a slick artsy style, à la Helmut Newton or the like.

Yeah, Lucien and I partook of many of the same scenes as the Book candidates, but we didn't put in anywhere near the effort, nothing approaching their constant networking for information and entrée. We kept the scenes in their place as something you dabbled in but in which you stayed clear of full immersion. I had very mixed feelings about them. Sometimes the scenes involved genuinely interesting people and other engaging elements of the strange organism that is downtown New York society; other times, they were flat and inane. Sometimes, New York nights unfolded like a flower; other times, they stubbornly refused to blossom. The fun and excitement of the nightlife turned into boredom if you went to the well too often.

Lucien started out referring to our Turkish host as "Paparazzi" after the celebrity photographer in *La Dolce Vita*. But after I suggested including a prominent layout of him in the *Coffee Table Book*, we asked Azine what the Turkish word for slug was. She said it was *sul* or something like that, and from then we referred to him as Sully.

After the simple breakfast, most of the group drifted around the house to the pool; a few people went inside to crash in various bedrooms. Our quartet lounged around the pool for hours, soaking up the sun, recovering. I wished I had sunglasses with me, but who knew I'd need them when we embarked the evening before. We talked casually with the others, discussed club culture with the pros from Holland, checked out their women. The Aussie talked endlessly about surfing and how "stoked" he got from just about everything. At different points, each of our foursome went inside and found a place to doze for a while.

The housekeeper brought out a buffet lunch, consisting simply of a large bowl of pasta with tomatoes and an oil and herb dressing, along with fresh bread. Sully complained loudly that the fusilli wasn't *al dente* enough for him. I found it pleasantly firm.

We left late in the afternoon. As we drove back to Istanbul, Giles regaled us with a vivid fantasy he'd had of inflicting some ultra-violence on Sully. Next to the pool, a whitewashed stone bungalow served as a wet bar/changing room. Giles was in there alone with Sully, changing into a borrowed swimsuit, and I suppose Sully was exuding his sliminess. Giles said he'd had a flash of suddenly punching Sully in the face repeatedly, bashing his teeth in and then pissing in his mouth.

"Christ, Giles, that's disgusting!" I said.

Lucien laughed and said with his mock East End accent, "Sully prob'ly woulda luvved it. Bit of the old U.V. Woulda been grite."

"Righty, right, right, me old droogs," chanted Giles.

I had to acknowledge the idea was perversely amusing, however outrageous it was. The image was horribly vivid—cool shaded interior of the bright white cabana, Sully on the tiled floor, striped with sunlight from partly open venetian blinds, mouth agape with blood and urine and bits of teeth swirling around inside. Right out of early Martin Amis.

I was forty years old when Lucien and I were in Istanbul. He was twenty-six. We'd met and become friends a year and a half earlier. Yeah, I know, it's weird—a forty-year-old guy actively hanging out with a guy in his mid-twenties.

Why did I have such a friendship? Well, to some extent, for the normal reasons—we liked each other, had common interests, etc.—but it probably also had a fair amount to do with the fact that for the first twenty-nine years of my life, I didn't remotely have the life

I wanted. The palpable wrongness of those years left a gaping hole inside my person, an insatiable want. And I suspect that when Lucien came along, I was strongly drawn to the chance to unexpectedly and belatedly have the late twenties I wished I'd had. I was a prime example of a cultural phenomenon that emerged in force in the '80s—the middle-aged man trying to hang on to his youth by behaving like a boy half his age.

To a lesser extent, I may even have wanted to vicariously experience the first twenty-four years of Lucien's life, as they seemed considerably more interesting than the corresponding years in mine.

To complete the picture and be fair to both of us, Lucien had a ton of natural appeal, which I responded to, as did a lot of people. And despite our age difference, we had a genuine rapport. We were engaged and entertained by one another's personalities. In simplest terms, we had good times together.

From his vantage point, I'm sure he wouldn't have been interested in the mid-twenties version of me had he met that person. But the thirty-eight-year-old version of me that he met had acquired a take on life which he found interesting and accorded well with his own. He was mature for his age, and I immature for mine. Though now that I think of it, had he been a more seasoned veteran of life, he might have gotten past my transgression.

I know my fascination with Lucien seemed a bit

creepy to some, and I could see why, but it didn't feel that way to me. It wouldn't, though, would it?

I believe we had a genuine friendship. I've had more than a few good friendships, having long needed a support network that my family never provided. And my friendship with Lucien was one of the finest. He probably doesn't think of it that way, but maybe I'm wrong.

What I didn't realize until later was that filling the deep hole inside me wasn't really possible. However much I made up for lost time, my exploits would never truly be what the lost time would have been. I was older. The lost time was gone, and the make-up time would never really do the trick.

It's been suggested I'm a bit of a navel-gazer, and there's definitely some truth in that.

■ ■ ■

"Hullo, lover. Looking for someone, are we?"

CHAPTER 2

"**D**rop 'em, blossom. Show us yer growler."

Mock Cockney accent, exaggerated deep voice, cartoon lasciviousness. Signature Lucien. Lines that caught his ear, phrases, often said apropos of nothing, no context. Sometimes staying with him for a few days, sometimes woven in and out of his conversation for years. Absorbed into his persona, like the flaws in fine linen, a natural quality of the fabric, as fashionistas are fond of saying. He always seemed half-aware that his persona was on display, but was relaxed and natural at the same time. He was a performer. Mephisto. Gollum.

That particular line—"Drop 'em, blossom…"—Lucien picked up from a scoundrel named Bobby Stevens toward the tail end of his days at public school. Bobby S was an older guy, mid-twenties, local, a bit dodgy. Sold hash and other drugs. His crude personality had a curious appeal, especially for the aristobrats at the school, always on the lookout for a bit of the debauch.

One night, Lucien and a couple of friends went out with Bobby S to the new nightclub in town. It had been promoted as having a spectacular state-of-the-art laser show. They stood around in the flashing darkness, drinking pints and gin and tonics. Before long, Bobby S pronounced in his coarse lowlife manner, which Lucien later came to mimic so well, "This is crap! I've seen better light shows in the cancer ward at the Children's Hospital."

Yeah, I know—vile and disgusting, not remotely funny to most people. But the over-the-top outrageousness made it humorous to the young lads. And even many years later, when Lucien related the incident to me and we were both supposedly mature adults, the same atrocious quality made us laugh. We cringed at how out of order it was, but all the same we laughed. That's what we were like.

September 1993. Downtown Manhattan, around midnight.

Lucien and I stood behind his girlfriend, Sharon, at the entrance to Squeezebox, watching her successfully work the door on behalf of the three of us. The club was Friday-nights-only at a small venue called Don Hill's in the neighborhood with no name west of Soho. Sharon assumed with a pout her inalienable right as a sexy beautiful young woman to be admitted wherever she wanted. The doorman ushered us in. As we entered, Lucien and I trailed behind, and he said in his cigarette-hoarsened voice, "One thing I've always admired about Sharon is her club attitude."

I looked at him with a smile. "Yeah, all you ever shared was a taste in clothes."

My comment was lifted from a line in a Lloyd Cole song we both liked. And reflected a certain figurative truth about the nature of his relationship with Sharon, which he happily accepted.

He and I stood at the bar and ordered drinks. Sharon drifted over to the dance floor to do her sex kitten thing. I picked up the thread of our banter. "All he ever liked about her was her club attitude." He smiled.

I first met Lucien in February 1993 through my girlfriend, who shall go nameless herein and who was close friends with Sharon. Both young women were students at FIT. Sharon was from St. Louis, of all places, my girlfriend from Tacoma, though she usually said Seattle—a more sophisticated city and more cutting edge due to Nirvana and the whole grunge phenomenon. Sharon was twenty, my nameless girlfriend twenty-one.

After I'd been seeing my girlfriend for a couple of months, she decided she was ready for me to meet Sharon and her new English ex-pat boyfriend. We made plans to get together one evening at a bar called Fez, in the neighborhood realtors had recently named Noho. I'd heard plenty about Sharon—my nameless girlfriend was quite impressed by her, at least by her looks and how guys reacted to her. I'd heard enough to know she was full of herself. And I was sure my girlfriend had told Sharon enough about me for her to have heard me referred to as David numerous times.

Sharon and Lucien were already at the bar, and she greeted me brightly. "Hi, Dave."

And for some reason, instead of responding nicely to her attempt at friendliness, I said "id," phonetically finishing my name (and by coincidence, I think, alluding to the potent pleasure-seeking side of my nature). It was stiff and unfriendly of me, but something about her brought it out in me. She said "Dave," and I said "id." Which wound up pretty much summing up our entire relationship.

Later that night, we all moved on to a club aptly named Sybarite. I didn't quite know what to make of Lucien. I hadn't expected to like him because he was with Sharon, but I did. He had a handsome but weird face, was vaguely foppish in his dress. He seemed intelligent and well-read, was engaging, though I couldn't always follow his elliptical way of expressing himself. He had palpable charisma.

A couple of times in the course of the night, Sharon made a point of calling me "Dave-id," leaning hard on the second syllable. And every so often after that, when we were together, she would pointedly refer to me that way.

By the way, I'm aware I have issues with women. That's part of the story.

You can't really talk about Lucien without talking about his looks. They played such a large role in his life, in how people reacted to him. He'd walk into a room—a bar, a party, wherever—and people would notice him, wonder what his story was. You could practically see them doing it. Club and party promoters would spontaneously approach him to get his name and info for their invite lists to stylish events. As one of the Frenchies said, "Strangers walk right up to him in a bar or wherever just to try to get to know him. *Incroyable!*"

His head was shaped like Steve McQueen's, and he wore his sandy-blond hair clipped short like the iconic actor. For a few months during our friendship, he had his hair bleached blond, which usually looked silly on men, but to my surprise he pulled it off. Most of his facial features were slightly exaggerated—lips, eyebrows, cheekbones, ears, giving him a slight monkey face, like Mick Jagger or Willem Dafoe, a look the French refer to as *belle-ug*, beautiful-ugly. His nose, however, was classically shaped. I used to point out its perfect form to acquaintances and tell them a plastic surgeon had re-built it after a car crash during his Formula One race-driving days (a complete fiction).

His eyes were an arresting shade of light green. I don't usually notice people's eye color; I'm adept at looking at people's faces without meeting their eyes. He had a pale green T-shirt he used to wear in the summertime and in hot places, which matched his eyes exactly, making them even more striking. The irises were like a cat's in that they seemed to hold more light than normal human eyes; and there seemed to be an increased translucency toward the surface. When he gave a piercing look, it was like a laser from under his brow, and if directed your way, you definitely felt it.

And of course, there was the smile. The impish grin that seemed to almost have a life of its own, radiating over his face as if it was irrepressible. In my favorite incarnation, I referred to it as the Lewd Grin—a glowing manifestation of the comic crudeness that amused us both so much. He had the debauch in him, that boy, and occasionally it showed all over his face. For me, faces are the most interesting visual in this world, and Lucien had a great one.

He was six feet tall, wiry, with narrow hips and broad shoulders that made clothes hang perfectly. Unquestionably a bit of a dandy. "I'm a poser, and I don't care," he'd sing as he got ready to go out for an evening, echoing some forgotten English '80s band.

There was something vaguely creature-like in the

way he moved. It struck me in particular when I watched him walk down the slope of a beach to the sea and back up after a swim, in a baggy swimsuit with his hairless chest. He looked slightly simian, though quintessentially human. His knees and elbows were slightly bent out as he moved on the shifting sand, and his wiry body seemed to roll from side to side, especially when he ran. Though peculiar-looking, his movements were graceful. His feet made weird imprints in the sand, thin at the heels and splayed wide at the toes. I used to call him Gollum, and he would rub his hands together, look around furtively, and say with his best Peter Lorre, "Yes-s, my precious-s. Yes-s-s."

––––––––––––––––

Late June 1993. Evening.

Lucien had spontaneously assembled a half dozen people for a week-long visit at his family's vacation house in Majorca. His family wasn't there, of course.

I'd initially resisted going. Lucien and I weren't yet close friends, and I didn't know all the people going. Plus I was older than the others. But my nameless girlfriend really wanted to go, and I liked Lucien, so I came around.

We had a late dinner outside on the terrace, and as I'd had to do all too often over the previous few days, I listened to Sharon's inane conversation. She was a deadly combination of opinionated and stupid. Well, not exactly stupid, but definitely not remotely as smart as she thought she was and a bit challenged in her ability to make sense.

Someone brought up the book *American Psycho*, and Lucien said, "It was nowhere near as bad as the critics said. I thought it was dead-on about New York society. The obsessive references to designer labels and getting reservations at all the right restaurants, competing about business cards down to the tiniest detail—all that stuff was hilarious and razor-sharp about what New York has become."

"The book's disgusting," said Sharon. "Taking all those girls back to his apartment and killing them in those horrible ways. A nail gun? Bret Easton Ellis clearly hates women. He's sick."

"You haven't even read it," said Lucien.

"No," Sharon readily admitted, "but I read an article about it in *Harper's*. And I've heard people talking about it. It's disgusting. The detailed descriptions of how he kills people, especially women." She made a face.

"Oh, well, then of course I retract everything I said. I only read the book."

Sharon spluttered.

I didn't know him well enough yet to realize he may not have completely believed what he was saying, but in the face of Sharon's aggression, he defended his position admirably, running verbal circles around her casually and pleasantly, gradually making her furious. He was subtle though. It wasn't clear he was baiting her.

I'm not sure I even picked up on it at the time; it may have become clear to me later on, looking back. But he did have that hint of mischief that hovered about him so much of the time.

Lucien wrapped up, saying, "Patrick Bateman is my new hero. I predict he's going to be a cultural icon."

After dinner, we sat around in the candlelight and darkness, finishing off the Spanish red. Sharon announced she was going to model for us some vintage platform shoes she'd found on Portobello Road on her way to Majorca. She went into the house and came out with them on. It was a hot evening, and she was wearing only a bikini and a see-through sarong wrapped around her hips. The platforms were made of wood and were about five inches high, authentic clunky leftovers from the '70s. She proceeded to flounce back and forth across the terrace, exaggeratedly swinging her delectable hips as if on a catwalk. Vogue-ing—flashing her hand across her face and off to one side as she snapped her fingers, simulating a spark shooting through the air.

My nameless girlfriend exclaimed, "You go, girl!"

The whole thing didn't have so much to do with showing us the shoes as with us all taking a few minutes to admire her. And maybe even desire her.

It was harmless enough. Something every attractive young woman should be indulged in every so often—flaunting her stuff, exuding her femininity. But for some reason, it irked the shit out of me even as her brazen sexiness completely worked on me. Maybe *because* it worked on me. But also because she so transparently thought of herself as a star. Not someone who had the potential to become a star, but rather somebody who already was a star. Admittedly an undiscovered one but already recognized in certain hip downtown circles for her star quality rather than any specific talent. She was, of course, deluded. She was extremely beautiful and painfully sexy, and yes, she might be able to parlay that someday into a facsimile of stardom for a few fleeting moments. In the end, though, it would only take her so far. And I suppose I found myself wanting her to find out the hard way.

Later in the trip, I said to my girlfriend, "She doesn't *deserve* to be around interesting, quality people. I mean, there are five other people here who have substance, each contributing in their own way to a good time. But she's just a drag on the proceedings. She manages to be consistently annoying. She doesn't deserve to be part of the group." That, of course, ignored what she brought to Lucien in the bedroom.

My girlfriend got what I was saying on a certain level. She and Sharon had a complicated friendship, as is often the case with attractive young women, especially when one of them is a real standout.

———————————

July to September 1993.

If Lucien hadn't gradually allowed me to talk candidly to him about Sharon, we wouldn't have been able to become such close friends. At the outset, I thought that was going to be an obstacle. But while he never came right out and said it, he let me know he saw her for who she was and knew why he was with her. Not that he wasn't caught up, but still he knew.

————————————————

Lucien wasn't typically English. I lived in London for a few years in my early thirties, and came to the conclusion that I didn't like English people in general, as later I was fond of telling Lucien and announcing to others in front of him. For many of the reasons people often give. In particular, the English don't like personal conversation. They'll engage in it guardedly when necessary but don't welcome it as interesting discourse and certainly don't seek it out, not the way neurotic New Yorkers do, all the Woody Allen types of my town. And they don't realize that life is meant to be enjoyed; they think it's only meant to be endured. A lot of negative energy on that dreary island.

Lucien's father had been a diplomat of some sort, and Lucien spent much of his childhood in Peru and later India. His family returned to England when he was about ten. When I got to know him, if the subject of his home country came up, he was scathingly critical, and often said he didn't think he could ever live there again.

———————————

Early July 1993.

Lucien's parents once caught a glimpse of what he was dealing with in Sharon. After the Majorca trip, he and she went to his parents' house in England for a couple of days. From there, he was going to Germany to rejoin the touring theater company he worked for at the time, and she was going back to New York. Her flight was a day after his, and she stayed on at his parents' house for the extra night. His parents had dinner with her at home and afterward politely sat and talked with her in the drawing room. In the course of the conversation, his father commented that New York could be very expensive, especially for young people.

Sharon responded with pride, "Oh, if you know how to act, you don't have to pay for anything." His parents later told him that upon hearing this, they became a bit concerned for him.

———————————

September 1993. New York City.

A few months after the Majorca trip, Sharon had her tongue pierced. Piercings in odd places were something you saw occasionally at the time, and I wasn't shocked, but it did strike me that this was a *hole* in her tongue. It seemed a bit excessive just to get some attention.

After that, whenever she wanted to turn a guy on—any guy, anywhere—she'd make sure he caught a glimpse of the little silver ball glistening in the middle of her moist tongue. Hey, it always worked for me.

One of the gang in Majorca was Matthew, a friend of Lucien's from New York, thirty years old, an actor, mostly in avant garde theater. It took a few days, but I came to like him during our week on the Spanish island. Back in the city, I asked him what he'd thought of Sharon's performance with the platform shoes. "Didn't you think she was ridiculous?"

"No, I actually felt bad for her, but," he smiled, "I always love encouraging Sharon to do just about whatever she wants."

October 1993. New York City.

My nameless girlfriend temporarily dumped me for making her feel bad about herself, and I took it badly, however deserved it was. Not long after Majorca, my friendship with Lucien had become independent of my girlfriend's friendship with Sharon, but even so, when I called him on a Sunday morning the day after it happened, I wasn't entirely sure how he'd react.

We met at Felix in Soho and sat at the bar off to the side of the Euro-brunch crowd. We sipped coffee and orange juice and talked. He said, among other things, "David, come on. She's twenty-one years old. You're thirty-nine. The relationship has a limited lifespan no matter what. And you don't really want it to be long-term. There's going to be stuff that comes up when you're dealing with someone that young, such a big age difference. You shouldn't be swimming in those waters if you don't want to deal with the currents."

We wound up walking around aimlessly for a few hours, talking more. It was an abysmally gray day. He didn't seem to mind that I was dispirited; he seemed to still enjoy my company. That may not sound like a big deal, but in my experience, a lot of people don't like to be around somebody when they're down. In the last several decades, there's been a distinct premium placed on being upbeat all the goddamn time. Myself, if I enjoy someone's personality, I usually enjoy it in all moods, good and bad (although recently I read that we have a moral duty to be cheerful, which got me thinking). Putting that aside, it's always interesting to see who comes through in the crunch and who doesn't. Lucien and I had a somber but enjoyable day. In some ways, that was the real solidification of our friendship.

What was so wrong with my first twenty-nine years? Basically, I would have liked to start over, but of course couldn't.

Like most young people, I didn't know who I was and for that reason, among others, wasn't able to conduct my life in a way that reflected my true nature. If you don't know yourself, it's almost impossible to make sound life decisions and build a satisfying life. On top of that, I felt I'd been born into the wrong place, the wrong family, the wrong situation. I didn't fit into the life I'd landed in via birth; it wasn't my home. And I spent my first twenty-nine years trying to find my way home. My actual life didn't remotely satisfy me, and I felt there had to be a life out there that suited me better. This other life, I imagined, was a rarefied one in which I had all the advantages of growing up in a privileged cultured worldly family. Enlightened. Though, of course, not so rarefied as to be snobby. Yes, that's pretty much what I wanted.

In the course of my floundering attempts to put my wrong-feeling life behind me and attain the life I wanted, I tried on a number of different personas, most of which were phony or misguided and involved badly flawed concepts about what was important in life.

At twenty-nine, however, through dint of what felt like super-human efforts over the years, I finally popped out of the end of the long dark tunnel and slipped into my real self, became who I genuinely was. I achieved a life that was true to my nature and possessed most of the qualities that the missed advantages would have served up.

And then my life began. Late, but it began.

What I didn't have, though, and would never have, was my first twenty-nine years the way I wanted them.

October 1993. Another Friday night, downtown Manhattan.

Sharon wanted to go home. Lucien didn't.

It could easily have been the other way around. Sharon was definitely a party girl, and usually ready to go all night. But that night she wanted to go home. Maybe she was tired, or maybe she wanted to be alone with Lucien. She was temporarily in between apartments at the time and was staying with him for a couple of weeks. But Lucien was in the mood to stay out, maybe go to Squeezebox later on.

We were at a birthday party for Peggy aka Piggy in the upstairs room of Flamingo East. The whole zoo was there, people from Lucien's and Sharon's circles. Doug the Slug; fey Billy Ferris, who wasn't as superficial as many of the others; Ruben, the trendy Korean painter who always had ecstasy; Carmen, Ruben's petite doll-like Cuban girlfriend who never had anything to say; Judy, the dull plain chick who worked at Vogue and was always around and nobody wanted to sleep with;

Katrina, the pixie-like half-Filipino stylist of ambig-uous sexuality; Trey, the diminutive gay black fashion designer; Justin, a strikingly handsome gay guy who was a salesperson at Barney's—he told a few of us that night how he'd been a high school football star, and for our amusement instantly transformed himself into the macho all-American guy he'd been. The transformation was amazingly complete and convincing.

Yes, I was quick to deride most of them, and yet there I was with them. What did that say about me? They weren't that bad, of course. Just young people trying to have their turn in the New York scene. But they had so little to say beyond their hipster reference points. I could never get a meaningful conversation going with any of them. I guess that was one of the prices I had to pay for being shallow myself.

My nameless girlfriend had left the party early—she had to be at work early the next morning as a sales-person at a Soho clothing store called *If*.

Sharon *really* wanted to go home and really wanted Lucien to come with her. Maybe more, she wanted to get her way. She didn't like having her will thwarted. And Lucien really *didn't* want to go home. Sharon's insis-tence only hardened his position. (As Giles later said at the Bar of Unnatural Blondes in Istanbul, the basic issue in any romance is who gets to be more selfish and by how much.) Anyway, Sharon was pushing hard, and discord loomed. She and I were being friendly to one another for a change, and if I remember correctly, she semi-appealed to me to influence Lucien her way. To flirt with her a little, I said to him, with her listening, "You've got to be crazy not to go home with her." She gave him a meaningful look making it eminently clear that untold delights were in store for him if he relented.

Soon, full-scale dissension made its appearance on the scene, and I don't know why, but I decided to try to play peacemaker. Maybe I thought Lucien would have an especially wild time if he went home, or maybe it was just to keep flirting with Sharon. As she faced him giving him a willful look, I whispered in his ear, "You should go, man." He didn't respond and looked at her with as much resolve as ever. She put her hand on his crotch and began to massage. He smiled at her in a strained way and shook his head firmly. "I'm going to get another drink," he said, and walked away.

She was visibly displeased, but surprisingly seemed to take the rebuff in stride. Maybe she saw it as only a temporary setback, or maybe she wasn't in the mood to make a scene. I wandered out onto a nearby balcony overlooking Second Avenue to get some fresh air.

When I came back in, she was standing where I'd left her, and instantaneously sidled up to me. She slipped one arm around my back and put her other hand on my chest, pressing her small but firm breasts into my arm. Most inflamingly, she lodged her mound of Venus against my upper thigh, and I think she even lifted her right leg off the floor and hooked it around my leg for a few moments. I felt uncomfortable, but tried to act as if she were just being friendly, and put my arm around her shoulders in what I hoped looked like a platonic way. I was acutely turned on. There was zero choice in the matter.

I glanced around the crowded room for Lucien but didn't see him, figured he was at the far end of the long narrow space, maybe deliberately staying away from her. She nestled up against me, blatantly rubbing her warm crotch against my thigh. She opened her mouth slightly, coyly revealing the tiny silver ball glistening in the middle of her moist pink tongue. It felt like steam was blasting up my spine and shooting out the top of my head. The girl was potent and knew it. She was obvious in the extreme, but that didn't matter one iota to me. I was rock hard.

She laughed and said, "You've never seen me really drunk before, have you?"

"Uh, well, maybe not."

I stood there, torn. I don't usually have much in the way of morals, but this was the girlfriend of my close friend, not to mention my girlfriend's best friend. I stood there throbbing for several long moments, then dropped my hand to her lower back and lightly pressed her against me. She wiggled, and I almost…I don't know, lost it.

I took a deep breath to clear my head, looked at her

with a strained smile, and said with a firm shake of my head, "You're the devil."

She laughed as if to say, *Who, me?*

I managed to continue to look at her with friendly disapproval, and she backed off, laughing a little awkwardly.

Lucien showed up a few minutes later, and eventually we all went home. Without any stops.

■　■　■

"That inconsequential, infinitely powerful creature: a pretty girl."

CHAPTER 3

Just before Lucien left New York to spend the rest of the summer of '94 in Europe and eventually Istanbul, he managed to get his hands on a copy of a book he'd been wanting me to read: *The Wasp Factory* by Iain Banks. He'd mentioned it to me a number of times as a book that had a large impact on him in his teens. It was out of print in the United States at the time, and his own copy was back in England, but he managed to borrow a copy off an English friend of his living in Hell's Kitchen, a struggling actor who was the male half of a couple we referred to as Pussy and Whipped. Whipped had a policy of never lending books, but Lucien prevailed on him to make an exception.

I went by Lucien's apartment to pick up the book the day before he left. He was living in a grotty loft on

17th street with two of the Frenchies. He handed me the book and said ominously, "Beware of *The Wasp Factory*."

The book was about an extremely disturbed teenage boy who, for obscure reasons, had been kept in relative isolation all his life by his father in and around their remote house on the Scottish coast. The house had an attic reached by ladder stairs, the youth's private domain; and a constantly locked study, the father's. At different points in the course of the boy's young life, he had killed three other children in bizarre gruesome ways, one of them his younger brother. Without detection.

Told from the viewpoint of the demented adolescent, the book places the reader inside the mind of someone who's not only young and psychotic but who's also been warped by isolation, stunted development and other unclear factors. The uniquely off-kilter internal voice of the boy speaks silently in your brain, eerily, sounding oddly normal at times and yet at the same time distinctly off. The reading experience was strange and disconcerting.

I tend to like disturbing art—films, books, paintings, music. Such as the more nightmarish songs by The Cure. Works that probe deep inside you and push the *disturb* button, triggering potent sickening feelings that you aren't able to experience in real life without the real-world horribleness that triggers them. I was fascinated by the book. It put me in a macabre world unlike anything I'd ever encountered before, in fiction or life. I wondered what had made the book speak so strongly to Lucien. Since he was moving around Europe at the time, I didn't get a chance to ask him for a while.

I started to toy with the idea that Lucien was secretly disturbed and was luring me to Istanbul to kill me as part of some twisted pursuit of experience or *sensation,* as he would put it. I let my mind run with the idea, and in my head blended *The Wasp Factory* with another novel and film that had strongly intrigued both of us—*The Comfort of Strangers*. An older Italian gentleman and his wife are living in Venice and insinuate their way into the holiday of a young English couple visiting the magical town. Their sole purpose, it turns out, is to experience the ultimate in sadomasochism by killing someone in an erotic context, in this case the exceptionally handsome boyfriend (played by Rupert Everett in the film).

What made me have these thoughts? What makes anybody think anything? Thoughts of all kinds slip into people's heads. Think of the sheer number of thoughts people have in a single day. I've always been a day-dreamer, taking visceral pleasure in letting my mind wander and drift. Also, it may have had something to do with wishing I was a writer—spinning out interesting scenarios. And seeing my life as a movie as some people tend to do. Maybe most of all, though, it had to do with my ongoing yearning to escape the ordinary, my deep want for my life to be keenly interesting. Of course, imagining being killed by a friend may have been going a bit far, but hey, I was just musing. And another factor may have been guilt.

It was an entertaining line of thinking, and after I arrived in Istanbul I joked with Lucien about it. He smiled and pointed out that nobody back in New York knew where I was. At his request, I had told everyone I was going to Cyprus.

You see, Sharon knew that Azine had been Lucien's most recent girlfriend before her and had moved back to Istanbul, and he didn't want to deal with the issues raised by that. This makes Lucien sound a bit shady, and maybe he was, but it wasn't that simple. Lucien had gone away for the rest of the summer without making any plans for Sharon to join him, and a big part of the reason was to put some distance between him and Sharon. He'd been exploring the idea, mostly in his own head, of extracting himself from their relationship. They'd been going out for over a year and a half, a bit longer than I'd known him. And as I learned later, his strong natural inclination, if he decided to end things with a woman, was to find a way to ease himself out. If possible, to orchestrate it so the two of them just naturally drifted apart until the break-up became little more than a confirmation of what already was. This could be seen as cowardly, but he said he liked to end things "diplomatically", so the woman didn't feel rejected. Give her a chance to salvage her pride. Minimize the ill will.

Anyway, it wasn't definite—ending things with

Sharon—and he didn't know what the nature of his hanging out with Azine was going to be. So, the story he and I sorted out was that I was meeting him in Cyprus. We figured we'd probably have to include Istanbul in our story when we got back, but we could make it seem as if we spontaneously decided to take a ferry to the Turkish mainland after I arrived. Lucien was fairly confident that Sharon and my girlfriend's knowledge of geography didn't include Cyprus being half Turkish, so it wouldn't occur to Sharon that he was going to Turkey. He was just putting off dealing with the issue, not expecting to avoid it altogether.

So no one in New York knew I was in Istanbul. And it became a running joke that Lucien had lured me there to kill me as part of some perverse sadistic game.

Charisma—it's a weird thing. I mean, what is it exactly? An intangible quality that draws people to you, completely separate from whatever other specific appeal you may have, such as wit or good looks or affability. By definition, charisma is something you can't put your finger on. It's pure personal magnetism floating in the air around the person, abstract from everything else likeable about them. And it's inherent—you either have it or you don't; there's no learning it, no way of getting it if you're not imbued with it early on. It's sort of amazing when you think about it—something that attracts people to you without any basis or reason. Must be a fantastic thing to have.

An intense example can be experienced when you go to a good concert and the front-man or woman, usually the lead singer, is powerfully compelling and completely commands the stage. Like Richard Butler of the Furs. In his prime, when I saw him going full throttle, I was absolutely riveted, couldn't take my eyes off him. He made me feel like a fourteen-year-old again, pumped full of euphoria and power and most of all dreams. At those moments, he was the fucking coolest guy on the planet as far as I was concerned. I knew it was just a feeling, prompted partly by certain cues, but I embraced it. Because humans need inspiration, and to not go with your enthusiasms is a fool's game. To be too cool for school is pure folly.

Lucien let his charisma do a lot of his work for him. I mean, he could be quite charming, but he didn't try to attract people. He let people come to him. And come they did. The whole thing was fascinating to watch.

Back when I was in college and yearned to be, oh, so world-weary and cynical, I taped a piece of paper on my dorm room wall with a line from a song. "Once I was a young man and thought all I had to do was smile." I wanted it to be true of me, but it wasn't. For Lucien, though, it was true in spades.

His charisma wasn't entirely a good thing. Things came too easily to him, doors opened too readily. He policed himself, kept in mind what was important in people, between them. But it is corrupting—people being drawn to you, indulging you, for no particular reason.

I occasionally wondered whether his charisma would fade somewhere down the line, and the famous Dylan song came to mind. *"Once upon a time you dressed so fine...gone to the finest school all right...but you know you only used to get juiced in it...All the pretty people drinking, thinking they got it made...You used to be so amused... How does it feel? To be on your own?"*

"So, have you fucked her?" Giles asked me.

He and I were sitting at the Bebek Café talking, playing backgammon and drinking Turkish coffee. It was early evening, my third day there. Lucien and Azine were at her apartment around the corner taking a nap, probably combined with afternoon sex. The café was a local spot, as was the village though part of the larger city. The village main street was part of the coast road running along the western shore of the Bosporus, and to get to the café, you turned off the main street and walked down an alleyway to the enormous saltwater river. The café was on the left facing the water. It was a basic place, but that was what made it so perfect.

The enclosed part had wood-framed windows running continuously along the two outside walls, letting in plenty of light. It tended to be full of older Turkish men playing serious games of backgammon at incredible speed. The constant clicking of pieces and almost continuous rattle of tiny dice created a pleasing rhythm. One of the ubiquitous framed pictures of Ataturk hung on the faded pistachio-green wall, and on the counter was an ornate antique coffee-making machine, which still worked, producing the extra-thick Turkish variety.

The outdoor terrace looked out over the dark waterway and was shaded by a translucent roof covered with vines. In one corner, an exceptionally gnarled tree rose through the roof, with its dense green branches spreading out above. The call to prayer came five times a day from the small mosque across the alley, another rhythm of the place.

As Giles and I talked, it was still light out, though the sun was on its way down over the hills behind the town. Across the water, an early moon was faintly visible against the cobalt-blue sky, hanging low over the Asian hills on the far shore. The light had a soft exceptional quality; the air was strikingly clear.

Though he hadn't initially struck me as the academic type, Giles was starting a doctorate program at Cambridge in the fall. In psychopharmacology, of all things. The big dilemma in his life at the time was that his girlfriend—ten years his senior, thirty-six—was pregnant and had told him she was going to have the baby whether or not he saw himself sticking around. Lucien and I both felt fatherhood was definitely not the way to go for Giles at this stage of his life, however painful and complicated it might be to avoid. But Giles didn't see it that way and was very close-minded on the subject, even with Lucien, despite the turmoil he clearly felt inside.

We were talking about Sharon. Giles had met her when Lucien brought her to England the previous summer, on the same trip that resulted in the vintage platform shoes being transported from Portobello Road to Majorca.

"What did you think of her?" I asked.

He made a face. "I've known Lucien since he was ten," he said, "and he's always had girlfriends who were dead cool. I can't figure out what he's doing with her. She's completely vacuous. I mean, I can figure out why he's with her because it's obvious. She's a dirty girl. But having a full-on relationship? For a long time? I don't get it."

"Neither do I."

"She's so…so provocative."

"Yup," I said.

"She demands attention from everybody…including Lucien's friends."

"Yup."

It seemed that neither of us wanted to come right out and say what an incredible flirt and tease she was because it seemed as if that should be embarrassing to Lucien, though it never seemed to bother him in the slightest. Then we dropped the facade.

"She comes on like a million volts to just about every guy she comes across," I said.

Giles nodded. "It's hard not react to," he said with a shake of his head.

"Yeah," I said grudgingly.

And that was when he asked. "So, have you fucked her?"

"No!" I exclaimed, taken aback that he was so ready to think I might've. And maybe for other reasons as well. "That's a rather cynical view of friendship," I said, partly to dissemble. But I knew all too well that human nature served up a good amount of reasons for thinking the way Giles did.

I sipped the last of my coffee and turned over the small cup to let the residue trickle down inside to form a pattern on the saucer that, according to Turkish custom, would foretell my future.

My girlfriend, who blew hot and cold on Sharon and saw her clearly to some extent, said of her once, "Sharon's the type of girl who's got to give a hard-on to every guy she meets. If she goes to the deli for a pack of cigarettes, she's got to give a hard-on to the old Puerto Rican guy behind the counter."

I know I'm making Sharon sound a bit one-dimensional, and I suppose there was more to her than that, but in a way she really was. Her sexual persona dominated her presence, permeated everything about her. It was always there.

She had it turned on all the time and not just a little bit. It hummed in the air around her. My girlfriend's roommate, who was a homely overweight young woman, once said, "Every time I see Sharon, I know she's gonna sex me up."

And that captures perfectly the way Sharon exuded sexual energy to just about everyone she encountered, especially in the first few minutes. Men and women alike, though men more, of course. It was her way of relating to people—her currency, her medium of exchange, the thing about herself she felt was of the most value. And above all, it was her power, her way of being in control, holding sway.

I walked into a bar with her once, with some others from our circle, and felt almost physically a wave of instantaneous sexual alertness ripple through the predominantly male crowd. She was giving off an exceptionally potent vibe that evening, like a scent, and the hounds picked up on it. She luxuriated in the experience, in her aura, even as she blanked every man in the room with authority. She was in her glory.

Yeah, she was sexy. I'll give her that. But it was too

much. Too constant, too blatant, too knee-jerk. Too physical. She had this signature way of standing, and when I think of her that's how I visualize her. It's seared into my psyche. She'd be talking to you, and if she knew you, or even if she didn't but was in the mood, she'd start standing close—I mean, *close*—and edge off to the side, turning her hips out slightly, so she was sort of simulating being wrapped around your thigh from about six inches away. And if she was really in the mood, she'd start moving her hips ever so slightly from side to side. Undulating. You think I'm exaggerating, but I'm not. This could happen to almost anyone—a downtown hipster, a flaming queen, a homely young woman. Or her girlfriend's new boyfriend. And it could happen just about anywhere—on the street, in a club, or in my kitchen. She did it instinctively. I'm not sure she was even always aware of it, though she certainly was sometimes. And if you were a guy, it could make rockets go off in your head. I mean, serious pyrotechnics lifting off at the base of your spine and exploding in brightly colored sparks at the top of your melting short-circuiting brain. The whole thing was bizarre.

Alongside her whole sex kitten act was her fashion statement—basic flash-and-trash—and she constantly flounced around to get attention. (A fulsome word—flounce.) She was completely over-the-top, cartoon-like, Barbarella to the hilt.

One of the strange things about her trip was her

limited comprehension of how people saw her. She thought everybody was awestruck by her, at least on some level, and certainly there was some of that. To be more precise, though, somewhere inside she *was* aware that a lot of people saw her in a negative light, but she just thought they were wrong. She thought really cool people could see that her way of conducting herself was all a hip outrageous act, that she was a feline star with loads of status in the clubs, entitled to behave however she wanted. People who thought poorly of her, to her way of thinking, just weren't cool or were jealous or both.

Maybe she was right to some degree. And maybe she was entitled, as a beautiful young woman, to be foolish and outrageous. On the other hand, there was no question that sometimes when you saw her in high gear, you knew you were watching someone who wasn't altogether right in the hea. There was something damaged, malfunctioning, a screw or two loose.

She had no wall up. Most beautiful women, especially in New York, have a wall up, a shell around themselves. They have to. Men come on to them constantly and would come on even more if they didn't radiate some standoffishness, some un-approachability. But Sharon didn't. Her walls were down, her receptors wide open to all admiration, desire, lust, from just about any source.

A gay fashion designer who knew her once showed me an elaborate color ink drawing he'd done of a highly stylized, beautiful, sexy witch—a Vargas-pin-up-girl-gone-fantasy-villainess. Complete with thigh-high black stilletto boots, long flowing white-fur-trimmed cloak, icy red-lipped face. A beautiful wicked enchantress from an adult fairy tale, embodying how the pull of pleasure can be heightened by the intertwine with evil. An alluring feminine creature beckoning you into darkness and flames. The fashion designer said that was how he saw Sharon. And *he* was someone who admired her.

She was a performer. A true performer.

Why did I dislike her so much? Was it because I wanted to fuck her so badly and wouldn't have stood a chance with her? Maybe. She was certainly out of my league looks-wise, and my appeal was not the type that worked on her. Maybe it was because she was Lucien's girlfriend, and I was jealous of her in the way that friends can be jealous. But however much those things may have played a role, there were more straightforward reasons. To use a hackneyed expression, Sharon and I were like oil and water. We were thrown together, both close to two of the same people, and had to deal with each other. If not for that, we'd never have had anything to do with one another.

Scorpio and Scorpio. Hey, she didn't like me, either.

I should say she never did anything all that bad to me, though I guess there were a few things. And she was young, which excuses a multitude of sins. I did think in the beginning she was going to hamper my enjoyment of others, particularly Lucien, but I found ways to work around that, just as she found ways to work around her dislike for me.

Ultimately, what I couldn't take was that she was so colossally and insufferably full of herself, expecting to be indulged at every turn. My indulgent side never made much of an appearance for her.

■　■　■

His husky voice whispered in my ear, late in the Turkish night, "Deeper. Deeper and deeper."

CHAPTER 4

"**D**avey the Bull. Davey the Bull Kebab." Giles chanted rhythmically from the passenger seat as we careened through chaotic Istanbul traffic. "Give 'em the horn."

I jabbed it sharply a few times as Lucien laughed in the back. I was far from alone in my use of the horn in the congested city. There was a cacophony of honking wherever traffic got hectic, and I happily followed the lead of the locals.

The nickname had sprung up over the last few days, having to do with my driving habits and a certain gastronomic sampling mission I was engaged in throughout the city.

I'm slightly embarrassed to say I didn't know it before I arrived, but the city of Istanbul is in two continents—Europe and Asia. The Strait of Bosporus divides the sprawling metropolis, running between the Black Sea to the north and the Sea of Marmara to the south. On the western shore is Europe, and on the eastern, Asia. The strait is about a mile wide where it passes through the city. Both shores are lined with hills, and the city and its dense array of buildings are oriented toward the water, so you're consistently looking out over the channel toward the other continent. I found this exceedingly cool, and in my first few days there I regularly pondered the phenomenon, swirling it around inside my head, thinking about what it had meant over the centuries. Right in the middle of the ancient city, the enormous body of land and throng of cultures that was Europe met the even more gargantuan body of land and throng of cultures that was Asia. The intrigue level for me, already high, went up a few more notches.

The European side is where the original city sprang up—ancient Byzantium, Constantinople. These days, in the stalls of the city's covered bazaars, you can find prints of detailed ink drawings of the much smaller city centuries ago when it covered only the hills around the Golden Horn, the enormous bay extending inland on the European side. A magical name, the Golden Horn, conjuring up all the enchantment and checkered past of the ancient metropolis.

We spent most of our time on the European side, as do most tourists, but late one night we took a ferry to a nightclub on the Asian shore. As we stepped off the boat onto the club's dock and took in the open-air night palace situated in its own wooded grounds, I realized with pleasure that I'd just arrived in Asia for the first time. The interior, it turned out, had a wildly sumptuous, ornate décor, with a super-abundance of pillows, illustrating that the phrase "fit for a sultan" had once had literal meaning.

The coast road on the European side ran along the shoreline for miles and miles, veering away occasionally. It was the main route through the city going north and south, and we routinely found ourselves driving on it at all times of the day and night. ("Give 'em the horn, Davey! Davey the Bull!") It was a deep pleasure to cruise along the shore through the city, and look out over the Bosporus in bright sunlight or sparkling darkness. The road and driving on it quickly became part of the fabric of our journey. Sometimes we drove along for miles, mostly within the city, occasionally into the outskirts.

I remember one night in particular. Late, driving slowly, almost no traffic. I was mildly stoned, nobody was talking. We were listening to the smooth moody sounds of Shriekback—crystalline surface notes against a lush background; the moody rich tenor voice—"Open up your filthy heart to me." I felt in every ounce of my being what a fine moment it was, and savored every drop—the enveloping night, my companions, Lucien especially, twinkling lights on the shores of two continents, perfect music, THC floating in my system, the pleasing sensation of the car winding its way along the contour of the coast. And on another level, the alienness of the situation, the ancientness, enormity, of the place. Being out there on the planet among it all, living life to the full, happy in both simple and complex ways. Feeling "right here, right now". However hokey that all sounds, however stoned, for me it was a moment of the type that life is about.

The moon over the Bosporus. I've heard people talk about the Havana moon, a harvest moon, a poachers' moon, and I'm sure there are plenty of others. On any given night, the moon can look pretty damn good just about anywhere. I remember one night looking down a side street in Greenwich Village and seeing a gorgeous orange almost-full moon hanging low between the dark silhouettes of pre-war buildings. But I have *never* seen the moon look as amazing as it did over the Bosporus. Glowing in the dark sky above the Asian hills across the way, its light silvering large patches of water. It was full on my fourth night there, and of course close to full the others. Every night it struck me anew, either from the balcony of my hotel room or Azine's balcony, or from an open-air restaurant or bar up on one of the hillsides. Or just cruising along the road.

The ships—enormous tankers, freighters—slipping noiselessly along as if in slow motion. Ferries, tugboats, motorboats, yachts. Early one evening, we sat on a low rooftop terrace/bar in the chic Ortokoi neighborhood, sipped cocktails and ate pistachios, as we watched the various boats go by and the sun went to hell. Minarets and domes punctuated the skyline in the distance. We took in the vast living panorama, and I had a powerful sense of the place having been one of the key crossroads of the world for thousands of years, a sense of all the vessels and people that had passed this way over the centuries. I thought I could feel the ghosts and reverberations from long ago. And here we were, passing through on our own journeys.

Our trip quickly took on a kaleidoscopic feel, a phantasmagoric roller-coaster ride. Azine was our guide and led us all over the city until late, very late, to places we'd never have found on our own. I drove, she directed. It was dark and foreign, labyrinthine, and we were usually under the influence of one substance or another, superb music pouring from the car stereo. Lucien, Giles and I often had little idea of where we were. We just plunged joyously along, looking forward to the next stop on the magical tour.

"Righty, right, right," whispered Giles reverentially.

We had drinks a few times at a spot we called the bar of unnatural blondes. Every country has its version of flashy bleached blondes—the St. Tropez look, curves on display, glittering gold jewelry. Turkey was no exception. We joked one night that Istanbul was a city where the women fully embraced being women, and the men had five o'clock shadows that just wouldn't quit. We were of course experiencing the cosmopolitan side of Turkey, by far the exception than the rule.

At a posh restaurant called Café Paris, we had dinner on a covered terrace built into a hillside, looking out at one of the enormous bridges spanning the strait, lit up like a diamond tiara. On a banquette off to our left, a beautiful Turkish child slept peacefully on richly colored cushions while his elegant family lingered over coffee and brandy.

We went to a partly gay bar one night where we ran into Sully and his supposed girlfriend with the lovely plump breasts. Lucien goaded me with his Cockney growl to go for it despite Sully's presence: "Come on, she wants to meet the beast. If Sully acts up, we'll give 'em a bit of the old U.V."

We were quite the hit there, especially Lucien dressed in an all-white suit and Giles with his long blond ringlets. Azine pointed out an older, conservatively dressed gentleman sitting off to one side with two handsome young men. She explained that he was one of the richest men in Turkey and most nights could be found out on the town looking for male company. We speculated what his liaisons might be like and how it all might come to a disastrous end late one night. Our collective imagination reeled.

Another night we wound up in the hills where the remnants of a castle in the midst of a pine forest had been transformed into a nightclub, a temple of

Mediterranean bacchanalia. *La Dolce Vita*, 1994. Spooky and fantastic. Crumbling old stone walls, towering trees, flickering candlelight from massive dripping cande-labra, revelers everywhere, long shadows. At one point, a Turkish pop band played in a courtyard fronted by a zany Middle Eastern drag queen. Lucien caught my eye late in the festivities and grinned. "Hey, just another Tuesday night in Istanbul."

I looked around turning his comment over in my head with an inward smile. In one sense, it seemed like he was just goofing—saying the line as a pretentious jet-setter might. But I knew what he really meant: "Hey, we're alive. Tuesday nights, in fact most nights, are usu-ally pretty humdrum, but tonight we're out here getting a taste of life. Living."

As we drove home late that night, a phrase caught my ear from the mix tape playing in the car, and I echoed it with a slight twist. "Lucien, someday your young veins will collapse."

With a mock-sinister smile, he responded, "Remember, no one knows where you are. Maybe there was a mix-up, and we never managed to meet up. I couldn't figure out what happened to you."

Azine. Resplendent Azine.

At Sully's pool the morning after the 2019 bacchanal, I lay on a blue-tiled bench, pillow under my head, feeling like a pool of melted butter. About seven or eight feet in front of me, Azine was languidly stretched out on a lounge chair, sunbathing topless. I still felt quite hazy, with the sensation of having been transported. I found it soothing to just lay there and gaze at this lovely creature with the Turkish moonscape as a backdrop—a perfect tableau. At one point, she rose from the lounge chair, walked over to the pool and dove in, barely disturbing the surface. I marveled at how this series of simple movements could be so completely imbued with femininity and grace, yet effected without the slightest self-consciousness. It was a human pleasure just to watch her.

A couple of days later, our Istanbul quartet was out at night at a subterranean Byzantine-style bar, and Giles and I stood off to one side talking, people watching. It was late, and I was mildly buzzed and tired from our frenetic pace. We could see Azine through a mosaic-covered archway where she sat casually on a sloped chair in profile to us, talking to someone out of sight, maybe Lucien. She leisurely smoked a cigarette. It was dark in the bar, but she was softly lit from some source.

As Giles and I talked, I fell into staring at her. We were in a shadowy spot, and even if she'd looked our way I doubt she'd have realized it was us or that I was watching her. It felt voyeuristic. Gazing at her mannerisms, her gestures as she listened and talked, her face, the nuances of her expressions; the way she held her cigarette, the easy movement of her hand and arm as she smoked; her smile and gentle laughter. A tendril of light brown hair swayed on the side of her enchanting Middle Eastern face.

At some point, there was a comfortable lull in my conversation with Giles, and we just stood there as I admired Azine, the silk-on-satin sounds of Bryan Ferry swelling through the room. Eventually I said with a shake of my head, "She's amazing."

Giles looked her way and said, "Indeed."

"Every one of her mannerisms," I mused out loud, "every gesture, is…is imbued with femininity and elegance. The way she holds herself. Even the way she smokes, and I hate smoking. She's completely nonchalant. She must have been brought up that way from an early age, and now it's second nature for her." I sipped my vodka tonic.

"Christ," I went on, "sexy and refined at the same time. Why don't more women realize they can be both, that the qualities can actually enhance one another? So many women think sexy equals trashy, that they have to choose one or the other. There's nothing in this world like sexy elegance or elegant sexiness." I trailed off, feeling a bit foolish.

"Did I ever tell you about Evie Cranston-Jones," Giles asked with a grin, "the upper-class slut from hell?"

I laughed. He had, quite graphically the day before.

You might be curious what Lucien did. I mean, how he paid the rent, how he filled his days in New York. Such things are essential to getting the full picture of a person. Some people may feel they're not important, or wish they weren't, but they're too fundamental to brush aside, they play too large a role in life. In a lot of countries, it's considered rude to ask somebody what they do. But Americans, New Yorkers in particular, are notorious for asking just that right up front. It tends to be how people define you in New York. In England, they define you by who you know, what circle you're in, where you fit into their highly stratified society. And they try to dance around the subject of what you do, for the sake of politeness, though that's been breaking down in recent years. Everyone's curious. As much as it might be commendable or interesting to get to know people without this information, to form your opinion about people based solely on more personal qualities, how a person pays the bills is too integral to not try and get a sense of.

People who met Lucien were often curious what he did, especially because it wasn't readily apparent. Sometimes when asked, he'd say, "Sweet fuck all."

I asked him once, "Just how sweet is this fuck all?"

"Sometimes it's sweeter than others," was his response.

Another time, I overheard someone ask him what he did, and he answered, "My best. I do my best."

People sometimes asked me what he did, and I went

back and forth between saying he was a dilettante and a lay-about. With warmth and humor.

When I first met him, he was working as part of management for a successful avant-garde theater company called *Dar a Luz,* though he had stretches of downtime in between productions. He went on tour with the company in Europe a couple of times— the get-together in Majorca had happened during a mid-tour break. Europe, I learned, has a large appetite for beyond esoteric theater and pays good money for it. For me, intentionally cryptic art is the refuge of the untalented, and I needled him about his involvement in inaccessible avant-garde theater. He tolerantly and knowingly indicated that I just didn't get it.

About a year after I met him, he quit the theater company because two of the key people he had to work with were too unpleasant for him to stomach. After that, he occasionally produced fashion shows and other elaborate events for companies on a freelance basis. He'd arrange the staging, décor, lighting, sound system, etc., and used crews he knew from the theater world.

Once he got a completely silly gig—a PR firm for Dewar's whiskey hired a gaggle of hipsters to get together for dinners at various trendy downtown boites and to drink Dewar's. In theory, they were supposed to brainstorm at the get-togethers about ways to give Dewar's a hipper image, maybe even help with the execution of an idea or two, but the reality was that they just had dinner and hung out and drank Dewar's. The Dewar's people were pushing something they called a Dewar's margarita, though how you can have a margarita without tequila escapes me. Lucien didn't really like Dewar's, and at one of the dinners he and another hipster—a so-called conceptual artist who made items like Chanel toilet paper, a Gucci handgun, a Louis Vuitton guillotine—concocted a drink called the Gallivant, consisting of a shot of Dewar's *alongside* a flute of champagne, which enabled them to drink champagne all night and poison the poor potted plant on the floor next to them. They even managed to convince others in the group that there really was such a drink, and soon had them ordering Gallivants and actually drinking them. The hipsters were each paid a couple of grand. It was absurd.

For the most part, though, after he quit the theater company, Lucien spent most of his time hanging out. He was a hang-out aficionado. Constantly going to cultural events—gallery openings, exhibitions, dance, theater, performance art, concerts, films. He read tons of books. A regular culture vulture.

But he didn't consistently do anything income-producing, didn't have any personal projects with serious scope, any focal point for his attention—that is, other than making sure his life was interesting. He believed that creating and leading a genuinely interesting life was a worthy pursuit in its own right. And he excelled at it.

Prior generations of his family, going back centuries, hadn't had to work, though a few had chosen to—*noblesse oblige* and all that. He once speculated that while his family recognized that times had changed and probably would have liked him to have a career, they would have felt guilty insisting he get a job. Not that he had limitless funds. His father was willing to indulge him, not encourage him. So Lucien hung out. With considerable aplomb.

When I'd ask him what he was going to do with his life or what his future held, he'd usually fend me off with a quip or jest. But late one night, at a party that was dying down, I said, "You know, you really should do something. Something you can sink your teeth into. I don't mean to be patronizing, but you're…you're too intelligent, too interesting—too interested in life—not to find something of substance to do."

He looked at me and said matter-of-factly, "Yes, I know."

What I do for a living is work as a businessman for a record company, Apex Music. I'm one of the point people for Apex in their business dealings with the outside world. I negotiate. Most often with artists through their managers and lawyers, but also producers and other companies. I go back and forth between the people who run Apex and the other side, trying to get a deal done that my side can live with. Professional interme-diary, high-priced messenger—that's more or less my function. Oh, and also, I'm occasionally one of the hired assholes—every company needs a few.

In my line of work, we refer to certain people as "closers".

There are some people who know how to close deals, and some people who don't. There are some people who know how to keep a deal moving forward, how to push it across the finish line. Who know how to cut through all the shrub-brush, who can readily distinguish between what really matters and what doesn't. Who are confident enough in themselves to be comfortable instructing their clients to sign on the no-longer-dotted line, and put the deal to bed.

And there are some people who don't have those qualities.

I'm squarely in the former group. I'm a closer. I know how to ride herd on a deal, how to ride it to the ground. I know the contract doesn't have to be perfect; it just has to work. I know the specifics of the contract rarely wind up being important; what's important is simply that the contract gets done so the record company has exclusive rights to the artist.

I know to subjugate my ego. I know to resist trying to be a hero. I know that sometimes the right decision is to agree to things that aren't remotely justified by concepts of reasonableness or fair play. I know there's *not* really a lot of justice in the world, and what goes around all too often does *not* come around. I know my job isn't very important. The talent-finders and, to a lesser degree, the marketing and promotion people determine the success or failure of a record company.

I know how to form an unspoken pact with the other side to help one another, to not crush each other as we do our work. I know how to firmly and convincingly let the other side know that my side has reached the limit of what it will live with or has concerns the other side can't ignore if they want the deal to happen.

I know that some days you eat the bear, and some days the bear eats you. I know that contrary to what some people think, compromise is *not* a vague psychological construct designed to allow weak people to explain defeat. And most of all, I know how to discern and figure out who has the *juice*, which is not always as clear as it would seem.

I am a closer. I have my flaws, but I know how to close deals. "They'll put it on your gravestone," a friend in the business once joked. "*He Was A Closer.*"

The term can be also be used in the context of sexual conquest. Where some guys fail to navigate their way through the oft-times tricky maze of erotic endeavor, the closer closes the deal.

The thing about Azine was that, on top of her many other appealing qualities, she was down to earth as well, and grounded. That was the crowning touch, the ribbon that tied up the package. I mean, how often do you come across a woman who's not only refined and sexy, but also real and stable? In my experience, refined, sexy and down to earth tend to each be exclusive of the other two. So, we're talking about a fairly rare creature.

She wasn't flashy or put together all the time. She was casual and relaxed, yet stylish and sophisticated. Eminently cool in my book.

She and Lucien were good together too. Comfortable and happy. He confided in me that they were having a great time in bed. There was something uniquely pleasing about her lips, he said, which he half-seriously attributed to the Arab strain in her blood. He told me a few months later that hanging out with Azine had helped make him realize that he shouldn't stay with Sharon. I gathered the only reason he and Azine had split up a few years back in New York was that circumstances had required her to move back to Turkey. Timing, life-paths, youth, lives yet to be led—all played a role.

I have a great photo of the two of them. We'd taken a ferry ride up the Bosporus to have a fish and raki lunch at one of the villages north of the city. It was a spectacular day—bright sunshine, saturated blue sky, cooling breezes. The vast dark waterway was spread out around us, green hills on either side, grand old Turkish mansions dotting the shores and hillsides. We passed under another of the enormous transcontinental bridges. I watched a group of dusky boys as they dove off a stone embankment, noisy and joyous.

In the photo, Lucien and Azine are sitting on the top deck of the ferry, open to the sky, both with sunglasses on, the wind whipping her light brown hair, him with his short-cropped look. They look beautiful. Not just their physical appearance. There's an inner beauty that comes through, too. Somebody I once showed the picture to quipped that it looked like a glossy magazine ad for designer sunglasses. And I suppose it does, but for me, the photo captures something well beyond the superficial. It conjures up a feeling akin to nostalgia, as if from another era. An attractive couple on the open deck of a ferry at an ancient crossroads of the world, an idyllic landscape as a backdrop, the two of them emanating a special connection and a zest for life. A time and place in two people's intersecting lives and everything that a moment like that can be.

On the penultimate evening of our trip, we were all at Azine's apartment getting ready to go out for the night. Peter Gabriel's *Sources* was playing on the stereo, with its strong Middle Eastern flavor. Her apartment was eclectically decorated in a rich Persian style, worn and lived in. Lucien and I were ready to go out and stood out on the balcony with gin and tonics, enjoying the music, the moon, the elevated view of the strait. I felt I could never tire of looking at the Bosporus. I took a few hits from a joint. He smoked a cigarette; he didn't enjoy grass.

We turned and leaned back against the railing, facing the ornate living room through a row of French doors. Azine came out of her bedroom and started casually dancing by herself in the middle of the living room. He and I watched her in silence, her lithe figure swaying to the music. If she saw us out there in the darkness, she took no notice.

I said quietly, "Look at her." Some wind chimes jingled faintly, blending with the music. "You know, you only come across a woman like that a few times in your life."

He smiled and nodded.

"Isn't it weird for you?" I asked. "Having great rapport, great sex with a fantastic woman, and not knowing when you'll ever see her again? I mean, how often are you going to find someone like her?"

He smiled his smile and said, "All is sweet."

January 1994.

Squeezebox again. Lucien and I had taken to going there regularly, usually with Sharon, sometimes my girlfriend, sometimes others from Lucien's and Sharon's circles. We wanted to partake of the place as much as possible while it was still delivering at peak level. Manhattan nightspots deliver the best version of themselves, hitting on a wide variety of cylinders, for relatively fleeting periods. (In four short months, 150 Wooster, like a comet shooting across the sky, went from being packed with the beautiful people to a place where you could roll a bowling ball the length of the room without hitting anyone.) Squeezebox was held in Don Hill's, which was not much more than a seedy glorified bar. Mistress Formika, a daunting drag queen, was the host of the Friday night soiree. The crowd was usually about eighty percent gay, with transvestites dancing on the bar and occasionally a young hustler type up there too, dressed in briefs and combat boots, always an attractive look. The women in attendance were powerfully alluring, almost without exception. Long a classic combination—beautiful women and gay men. As my girlfriend pointed out, an attractive woman could go to a mostly gay club like Squeezebox and dress and dance as provocatively as she wanted without being hassled by guys. On any Friday night at the time, you could see dazzling young ladies out on the dance floor dressed in only, say, a black bra, hot pants and platform heels, putting on a tantalizing show.

The unofficial house band at the time was a recently formed group called Nancy Boy, fronted by the it-boy of the moment, Donovan Leitch, named after his famous surname-only father. They played a passable '90s variant of '70s glam rock a la David Bowie, and reveled in their androgyny, though Leitch was a notorious womanizer, or to use the term Jack Nicholson coined, modelizer. Gaggles of stunning young women always showed up for the group's gigs. A pony-tailed music lawyer once described the band to me as "Ziggy meets Twiggy meets Iggy."

That night, I was there with Lucien, Sharon, and a couple of other scenesters. I don't recall why my girlfriend wasn't around. I was perched on top of the backrest of a metallic-red vinyl banquette, glittering slightly in the dark, my back against the wall and chelsea boots on the padded plastic seat. I think fey Billy Ferris was sitting next to me perusing the crowd. Sharon stood in front of me facing us. Lucien was in another room.

Sharon and I were making one of our attempts to have a sustained conversation, which stemmed from the fact that we were around each other a lot those days and occasionally had to make an effort in order to keep things comfortable. Also, I think once in a while she wanted to show she could have a meaningful chat with me if she wanted. After all, two of the people she was closest to enjoyed whatever it was I brought to our social swirl. For my part, I'd gotten to a point where I could appreciate her as part of a group; she definitely added spice to the mix.

I don't remember what we talked about above the din. It might have been a book, which would make the incident even more ridiculous. Sharon and I trying to have a cerebral discussion while…

It was, of course, dark and crowded. We had to lean toward one another to make ourselves heard. I began to feel her pelvis brush against my knee a bit more than seemed incidental. I didn't react. Didn't shift my knee either.

Gradually as we talked, neither of us acknowledging what was going on below, her contact with my knee became more frequent, more deliberate, until her crotch was simply lodged up against it. There was no pretending any more it wasn't happening. She was brazen. Amazingly brazen. I was extraordinarily turned on. Lights flashed and bells clanged in my brain like a pinball machine. But Lucien was a close friend and could have easily strolled up at any moment. Also, I disliked her, though that didn't seem to matter much where my cock was concerned. Maybe more to the point, I knew she didn't like me, wasn't especially attracted to me. But that didn't seem to matter either. If anything, our mutual dislike seemed to blend with the sexual flirtation in a way that made the situation more erotic. More raw, more potent. Like hate-fucking if you're familiar with the phenomenon.

We kept up the pretense of having a conversation, but it consisted mostly of just keeping words coming and hardly listening to what the other was saying but nodding anyway. Lots of nodding. I was at maximum arousal, and I'm sure she was enjoying herself thoroughly. Her effect, her power. I felt like she and I were *right there*, fully in the moment, in our own intense little vacuum. We looked directly into one another's eyes, something we rarely did, though mine were a bit glassy at the time. Challenge vibrated in the air between us, provocation. We were like two combatants circling one another warily. Scorpio and Scorpio. Aggression veiled in titillation. Complicity shimmering in the murky ether.

I gently began to push back with my knee. She responded with more pressure, rocking very slightly. I thought I might explode. My eyes rolled up inside my head.

Billy Ferris pulled his distracted gaze away from the milling crowd and interrupted us with some casual remark. The seal broke. Oxygen flowed back into our brains. We subtly disengaged.

■ ■ ■

Istanbul nights. Late. Very Late. His voice insinuated itself into my brain, with his best stage whisper, "Oh, the horror. The horror."

CHAPTER 5

Alex and Roddie Baines. People from Lucien's past. He didn't tell me the whole story all at once. I pieced it together over the two and a half years we were friends. And as the pieces came together, I gathered that most of his New York friends weren't aware of it.

Alex, short for Alexandra. She'd been Lucien's girlfriend in England for three years ending shortly before he moved to New York—from age nineteen to twenty-two for him. She seemed to be the one girlfriend in his relatively young life to whom he attached real significance. I saw a photo of her once, but it was early on in my knowing him, before I was aware of her import, and I didn't look closely. All I remember is she had straight dark brown hair and looked pretty.

They fell in love when they were university students

at Oxford. Giles was a student there with them, too. Lucien dropped out after a year and a half; I'm not sure why. He definitely kept reading and learning extensively, and when I met him, was better educated than most college graduates I knew. Alex was a year ahead of him and continued school to get her degree while Lucien stayed on in Oxford town hanging out. Then they moved to London together.

Roddie Baines was part of the aristobrat crowd Lucien ran with in those days. He was more or less a posh adolescent criminal. His grandfather was Lord Baines, whatever that meant, but his father was a second son and hadn't received much inheritance. What with that and the English aristocracy generally coming to the end of the line, Roddie Baines didn't have an abundance of funds. And he gradually turned to crime, though it sounded like it may have had as much to do with his wild boy personality as with a shortage of money. I mean, he was far from impoverished by most people's standards.

Lucien once said with some bitterness that Roddie was small and hideous. "But," he added with a grudging nod, "he had something. He was funny and witty, often in a nasty way." I think most people have known someone like Roddie Baines in the course of growing up—a kid who has magnetism but is bad news. Got out of line on a regular baais but was cool as far as the other kids were concerned, in part because of his daring misbehavior. And with a mean streak. In small-city Indiana where I grew up, these guys were usually hoodlums with some crude charisma. But I've encountered the well-heeled variey, as well, and they can be extra unpleasant— money can breed some really ugly behavior.

Roddie Baines started out with pranks, not that different from most of the kids in their youthful crowd, including Lucien. While some of the pranks were pretty outrageous, they stopped short of going beyond the pale. "It was funny at first," said Lucien. "You know, we'd be at a pub, and he'd steal some yuppie's handbag. Wouldn't tell anyone. He'd just buy drinks for everyone all night until somebody wondered about it. Giles might say, 'C'mon, Roddie, whad'ja do?' And he'd want to tell us. He wanted us to know. He'd think everybody was going to laugh and be impressed by his bravado.

"But he started to get stupider about it. I took him to a party once, and everybody there pretty much knew everyone else, except for the people I brought. And Roddie went through everybody's coats and handbags. People lost a lot of cash. It wasn't just some minor thing. I got confronted because people were convinced it was one of the people I brought. And it was."

At one point, Lucien was living with a group of five guys including Roddie, in a house on Becket Street in Oxford. Roddie would steal his flat-mates' vinyl records and sell them to the local record shop. Lucien found some of his in the used record bins, recognizing them from the felt-tip marking he'd made on them.

Lucien once brought Roddie to his parents' house near Oxford, and Roddie stole fifty quid from the cleaning lady's handbag. He took Lucien out for a nice meal with the cash before Lucien realized what had happened. When he did realize, he was furious—this was the cleaning woman, who wasn't well off and worked hard for her money. And on top of that, it was at his parents' house.

The Becket Street Binge. While they were living there, Roddie inherited something like twenty thousand pounds from a relative and proceeded to blow it all in about three months, taking his friends along for the ride. One could say that he was generous during the spree, but it was really more that he just spent wildly when he had money. He felt he shouldn't have to be concerned about money. He bought a motorcycle, flashy clothes, drugs, and he and his mates embarked on massively free-spending outings—big dinners, nightclubs, champagne.

And he bought a boat. To ride around in on the Thames. Nothing fancy, a stylish old wooden cabin cruiser. They would round up a bunch of people and have a drinks party as they cruised up and down the river, being swank and decadent. Not for long though. In the midst of one of their floating bashes, they were approaching a bridge. A couple of Roddie's guests pointed out it looked a bit low, but he shrugged them off and kept going along at a pretty good clip. Sure enough, the bridge sheared off the top of the cabin, bringing the boat to a grinding halt, throwing revelers to the deck. A few people dove off.

Roddie abandoned the boat, having exhausted his inheritance at this point. Had no insurance, of course.

There came a point when Roddie's pranks couldn't be dismissed anymore. When you hung around with him, you ran the risk of getting in real trouble, with cops involved, and even worse some seriously unsavory types.

Lucien and Alex were living together in London. She worked as an executive assistant at Virgin Records, and I think he actually spent a few months in some entry level position at a bank, as hard as that is to imagine. Things began to get stale between them.

Giles was still in Oxford, finishing up university, and proposed to Lucien that he come back so they could start a hip local magazine focusing on the abundant cultural life in the area, like a *Time Out* for Oxford. Lucien liked the idea and decided to give it a go, without working it out with Alex what it meant for them. In what I later learned was classic Lucien style, he left it up to her to decide whether she was going to join him or not. And didn't try to steer her either way. He actually moved back to Oxford with it still being unclear what she was going to do. She followed about a month later but was understandably unhappy with the way it went down. They moved into the ramshackle house Giles was living in. Roddie Baines lived a bit outside of town, getting up to increasingly shady activities.

Lucien and Giles threw themselves into starting the magazine, with Giles still having some academic demands as well. Alex made some half-hearted attempts to find a job but couldn't find anything comparable to the opportunities in London and fell into inactivity and malaise. The connection between Lucien and her diminished, and they didn't deal with it. Lucien began to feel a distinct weirdness in the air, and it felt like Roddie Baines was somehow involved.

One long weekend, some of their circle, including Lucien, Alex and Roddie, went up to the Lake District to stay at the country house of someone's parents. On the train there, the weirdness came to the surface, and Lucien could viscerally feel the complicity of Roddie. He cornered Roddie in the bathroom. "I don't know what you're doing, but I'll kill you if you don't stop." Completely unlike Lucien. Not only wasn't he the violent type, but he almost never lost his cool. He was trying to regain some control of the situation.

After they got to the country house, Alex proceeded to mess with Lucien's head for the entire weekend. And his guts. At the end of the weekend, when he was getting ready to leave, she announced she was going to stay on for another day or two with some of the others, including Roddie.

Lucien told me he felt his insides ripping apart and said to her, "Listen. We've got to sort this out between ourselves. This is *too* public. You've got to come with me to sort this out."

"No," she said in a toneless voice. "I'm staying."

When he told me about this, he said, "There are moments when you reach the spillover point of emotional breakdown." He was in deeper than he'd realized. His girlfriend and a friend of sorts were betraying him in front of a bunch of their friends. His ego had the raw power of a twenty-two year old's, engine roaring, intake valves wide open. His vulnerability was fully exposed. And he was winging it, not really knowing at the time how to deal with a situation like that, if one ever does.

"Humiliation is a real character builder," he said to me.

There was, of course, an epilogue, dragged out and painful. A tangential development was that Giles, Lucien's closest friend, chose not to cut back on his friendliness with Alex and Roddie. Myself, I think there are times when you've got to take sides. Lucien and Giles' friendship had apparently never been quite the same, though four years later we were all in Istanbul having a rollicking time.

I suppose the whole thing made me like Lucien more, knowing that his extreme self-assurance had been shaken severely at least once, that he hadn't always coasted through life with everything going his way. And his telling me about it, especially for him, was a genuine expression of friendship.

■ ■ ■

"Man is invisible until the cold waters of experience have shown him who he is."

CHAPTER 6

Early July 1994. The Hamptons.

"**A**llo, Chas. Oo do you think you are? The Lone Ranger?"
"Ee thinks he's Jack the lad."

Lucien had written out the quote in enormous letters in the wet sand. You had to walk forty feet or so along the slope of the beach to read the whole thing, unless you could've somehow managed to hover above it in the air, which is the way I always picture it—must be thinking of the camera shot for the film.

Over the previous few weeks, he'd regularly said those lines for no particular reason. Out of the blue. With feeling. Sometimes just part of them. It had proved to be one of his more enduring expressions. I'm pretty sure it had enjoyed a prior appearance in his active repertoire, and the current manifestation was a revival of sorts. He mimicked perfectly the growls and lower-class accents of two East End criminals talking to one another. He liked the sound of it—the picaresque quality, the inflections, the jargon. So he'd say it. Occasionally, I'd deliver the second line for him as the second speaker. Sometimes, he'd just say the first two words—*Allo, Chas*—stretching out the syllables, wrapping his mouth around the sounds, pronouncing them as broadly as possible. Curl his lips crudely at the end. Then maybe leer exaggeratedly for good measure.

The lines came from two elements of his personal pop culture, and coincidentally mine as well, though I can't say they'd leapt out quite as much for me as they had for him. They were originally part of the dialogue in a film called *Performance* starring Mick Jagger, and more significantly co-directed by two staggering talents, Donald Cammell and Nicholas Roeg. It's about an East End criminal named Chas, who seems to be going renegade vis-à-vis the criminal enterprise he's part of, or at least isn't following orders. He arrives at the gang's office one afternoon, after his colleagues have started to get suspicious of him, and two of the other heavies, stocky barrel-chested blokes dressed in dark suits as if they're legitimate businessmen, casually confront him with barely disguised menace. One of them says to him with a thick undercurrent of threat: "Allo, Chas. 'Oo do you think you are? The Lone Ranger?"

And before Chas responds, the other guy answers

for him, with dripping sarcasm, as Chas stands there wooden-faced. "Ee thinks he's Jack the lad."

The film has a small but avid cult following, and Big Audio Dynamite sampled the lines in their stand-out track, "E=Mc2," along with other gem-like snippets of dialogue from the film (like the Mick Jagger character proclaiming in a deep sonorous tone with a slow motion cadence, "I don't like music.")

I'd seen the movie about five times when I met Lucien, and he'd seen it several times too. And we were both big B.A.D. fans—one of the first bands to successfully blend rock and dance music, with irresistible results. Eventually, we rented the movie and invited a bunch of people over to my Tribeca apartment one evening to watch it. That was when the lines re-emerged in full force as part of his lexicon. You might think it would get irritating— the regular nonsensical repetition of a phrase or line, like an annoying child—but he had a large ever-growing catalog, and any one expression tended to fade away and get replaced by another before it got to that point. Though I have to say this one had a long run.

Enormous words in the wet sand. We were on the beach in Wainscott when he wrote it out like that. And if I'm not mixing up weekends, we were joyously tripping on mushrooms at the time.

I rented a house out there for several summers and usually invited various friends when I went out. Fortunately, my job at Apex paid well enough for me to avoid having to do a share house. It was key to my enjoyment of the place that I be able to pick who came and the combinations of people. Creating a successful gathering, especially for a couple of days, was like baking a cake. I went out there mostly on weekends, being a working stiff and all. After Lucien and I became friends, he and Sharon became regular guests. Those summers were superb—'93 and '94—blessed times when everything was going right, a period rife with good times that seemed like they'd go on forever, though of course they didn't.

The house was a five-minute car ride to the sprawling beach and the vast calming, though sometimes mercurial, Atlantic. It was deep in the Wainscott woods at the end of a long sandy-dirt driveway running serpentine through the trees with sunlight filtering through here and there. In a clearing with a deck and pool in the back, surrounded by seriously tall trees that seemed to almost always be swaying hypnotically in the breeze, rustling. A very pleasing sound—the rustle of leaves.

We had some times out there.

August 1993.

"You know, in the Amazon," Lucien said to my girlfriend, "you can't piss in the rivers because there's these tiny fish that attack your dick."

He was standing waist deep in the pool in Wainscott. She was laying in a lounge chair on the deck. Both were drinking Pimm's. I stood at the barbecue tending the chicken, mildly buzzed, half-listening. It was mid-evening; dinner was coming together haphazardly. Chryssie Hynde snarled gloriously on the stereo, *"I'm the adultress. I didn't want to be…"* Other guests were inside, scattered around the house.

"Yeah," Lucien said, "they're attracted to the urine."

As I turned the chicken over, I got the image of a guy treading water in a jungle river and pissing with dozens of vicious little fish nibbling away at him underwater. But no.

"They swim right into the Jap's eye," he continued, "and once they're inside, they sink these little barbs in."

The picture in my mind morphed into the same image but with dozens of almost microscopic fish finding their way into the guy's urethra and sinking barbs into the inner walls. But no.

"When you piss in the water," he said, "they swim right up your piss. They're used to swimming up rapids and small waterfalls, so it's like…"

The image clicked in—miniscule fish swimming up a yellow cascade into a guy's dick.

"You are *so full of shit*," I said, laughing.

"It's *true*," he said indignantly.

"Yeah, where'd you hear this?" I asked.

"It's a well-known fact, you ugly git."

"I love that form of argument. Whenever you're on shaky ground, assert it's common knowledge, and then throw in the old *argument ad hominem* for good measure. You ignorant slut!"

"Hey, just ask Matthew. As soon as I have a word with him." He grinned. Our friend Matthew was somewhere inside the house.

I shook my head, laughing some more. "Come on. Where'd you hear this?"

"I was born in the fucking Amazon," he said with renewed vehemence, alluding to his childhood in Peru.

My girlfriend sat there listening to all this, an amused expression on her face.

"Don't listen to him," I said to her. "He just makes this shit up. It's unbelievable. He makes it up, and then says it like it's…like it's a fact. And if somebody challenges him, he just digs in and talks like he's an authority."

I looked over at him and said, "You know what your problem is? You only argue to win. You don't care what the right answer is."

"That's the whole point of arguing," he exclaimed. "To win. What do you argue for?"

"I argue to figure out what the right answer is. I've got my position, and the other guy's got his. And we go back and forth trying to figure out what the truth is."

"The truth," he scoffed. "There is no truth. There's only my reality and your reality. Me trying to impose mine on you, and you trying to impose yours on me."

I could tell he was being provocative and didn't necessarily believe in what he was saying, but I could work with that. "Bullshit. There's a reality independent of people's viewpoints. And the point of…of debate is to try and figure out what that is."

"No. Arguing is about winning. It's about whose reality prevails."

I shook my head. "The point of debate is to achieve the correct understanding, figure out what the truth is."

"You're telling me you don't want to win when you argue?"

"Sure, I want to win. I get caught up. But winning's not the main thing. The back and forth of the argument pushes me to examine my position, refine it, maybe incorporate some of the other guy's thinking into mine. *Maybe* even change my mind. I'm trying to figure out what the right answer is. Hindered, like everybody, by my own baggage. My biases, defense mechanisms. But I'm *trying* all the same."

"So, you're saying you argue for the truth."

"Yes," I said, recognizing he'd managed to back me into sounding self-righteous. "And you argue to win. That's your problem."

He slowly clapped his hands several times, loudly, like gunshots in our woodsy clearing. Then he cupped his hands around his mouth and shouted toward the house for everyone inside to hear. "Let it be known that David Burdon argues for the truth."

When I first met Matthew at Lucien's house in Majorca, he was a bit standoffish. But he seemed interested in getting to know me and had an appealing quality, calm and soft-spoken.

Soon after we all arrived, I gathered he was completely immersed in what he referred to as "club culture". After dinner on our second night there, a few of us were standing around in the narrow messy kitchen, the big window at one end open to the night air. We were finishing off a bottle of red, and I asked Matthew bluntly, "Don't you get bored with the whole club scene? Is it really worth big chunks of time and energy? Really worth deep immersion?"

As much as I dabbled in the nightlife, the club scene is the late part, often very late, and involves a narrow spectrum of stimulation, generally excluding conversation. A steady diet of the club scene, three or four nights a week, would have been too much for me. My question to Matthew was a bit confrontational, but I wanted to engage him, see what he was like.

He responded in a roundabout pausing way, which later I became familiar with. "I like the theater of club culture. The theatricality of it."

I shrugged, acknowledging there was something to that.

"Most of all," he said, "I love the DJ'ing. It's a true art form when practiced by a master."

"Oh, come on." I smiled to offset my contrariness. "How much artistry does it take to play records?"

He smiled back. "You're wrong, man. A really good DJ can do amazing things. Not just musically. Atmospherically, building momentum, playing the crowd like an instrument. Taking the crowd on a ride. A great DJ can achieve complete control over a crowd. Dishing up euphoria, driving them into an ecstatic frenzy." He ran his hand over his shaved head. "You ever heard Junior DJ?"

"Maybe. Not that I'm aware of."

"Oh, man, Junior Vasquez. You should hear him. He DJ's with *authority*. Total authority."

Mathew said he DJ'ed himself sometimes. I soon stopped challenging him as much and just listened.

"It's a musical thing," he said. "A DJ has two turntables and an equalizer…and an effects unit for, like, reverb…He puts a record down, a record he loves, and that record is like the first word in a composition. It's like a canvas. He puts the record down, and it's like the beginning of an epic poem. And then he puts a second record down and it rides in underneath the first one, and he sees which one is working better, which one he wants to go with…

"He knows…He has a love affair with every one of his records. And every week he goes out and searches for more, looking for stuff that reflects his sensibilities. He takes them all and creates a collage that represents his sonic landscape. And it disappears into thin air. That's part of what I like—the fleetingness of it all.

"You make mix tapes," he went on. I'd brought some with me and played a few. "You know the gut-pleasure you get from listening to a great song, and the importance of having the right sequence. The DJ adds a technological understanding. It's a craft. How to pitch a song. How to play one right on top of another.

"A DJ extracts the most delicious elements of the music, when it's the right moment, taking the sweetest part of the fruit. And he creates a salad of the most delicious things…A DJ can change a recording, make you hear it in a new way. He'll take the very best part of the song, the part you love best, and he'll go on and on… play it over and over. Reducing the logic of the song, reducing the cerebral tendencies in people dancing, sending them into a sensual realm where nobody's thinking at all…

"Clubs—a lot of the impulse relates to the sexual instinct, only it's music. It takes the form of music. All sorts of desires and appetites are reflected in the experience. Hidden in the heart, at the core of a great record collection, is the Penis King. And a great DJ when he's playing at a club, when he really embodies the spirit of his record collection, he conjures up the force of the Penis King.

"You're the king of the crowd. And they're all receiving you."

"Allo, luv. Got any brothers?"

I never quite appreciated that line as much as Lucien, but I got a kick out of the way he thoroughly enjoyed saying it. Apparently, it was another Bobby S catchphrase. Bobby S, who wasn't the most savory of characters but was handsome in a rough way, would walk up to a bird in a pub or somewhere and say, "Allo, luv. Got any brothers?" The beauty of it, according to Lucien, was the odd confusion it usually caused in the woman. Did he mean he fancied her and was concerned about protective brothers? Or did he mean he was gay and would fancy a bloke who looked like her? Or was it just nonsense? It was a puzzling remark, vaguely suggestive, almost lewd, especially the way Lucien said it. It definitely had the sought-after vulgar quality we enjoyed.

Another signature expression. We'd be out in a bar or somewhere and a couple of women would walk in, one of them attractive and the other decidedly less so, and he'd say, in his East End accent, "Oo, don't like yours much."

It went on and on.

I collected shells and stones on the Wainscott beach during those summers. I did that in a lot of places I traveled to. Scattered around my apartment was a wide array of beach leavings. On my kitchen counter was a plate of blue shells from the vast wind-blown Dutch beaches on the North Sea. (In the sky behind the beaches, you could almost always see the puffy white cloud formations made famous by Dutch painters.) On a windowsill was a cluster of exceptionally smooth, pure white stones from crystal clear waters off a small uninhabited island in the Aegean. Brightly colored coral from the Indian Ocean were displayed on a small round side table. On the dresser were an assortment of glass and pottery fragments worn smooth by sea and sand, scavenged from a Caribbean beach where I'd gone to watch the sunset. All part of my personal tapestry, such as it is, occasionally stirring up memories, in the same way as a photo album or an old mix tape.

I didn't fully appreciate the appeal of stones until Matthew brought me once to visit a friend of his, an eighty-year-old Buddhist woman sculptor. She lived In a cavernous loft that served as her work space as well. At the base of one of the twenty-foot columns spaced around the room was a grouping of large smooth pleasingly-shaped stones loosely arranged on the wide-planked floor. I don't generally subscribe to mumbo-jumbo, but I could feel the zen-like effect of these stones.

It's not just the objects themselves. The act of finding and choosing shells and stones can have a zen-like quality, too. You wander along a beach, staring down at the scrabble of sea remnants endlessly washed up by the waves. Specific ones catch your eye, you pick them up, examine them. Keep some, maybe only till you get back to your towel, maybe for a lifetime—the real keepers. You can lose yourself in the simple activity, with large parts of your overwrought brain shut down and quieted for a while. A genuine relief. Calming, soothing. Kind of like the way I imagine gardening.

I also went through a phase of collecting interesting-looking broken shells. The openings left by the missing fragments revealed inner whorls and spirals, with the edges of the breaks worn smooth. Something about these fractured shells spoke to me—the way natural beauty acquires texture and detail through the forces of time and nature.

In the fall of '93, I bought a rock tumbler to try buffing some of the stones, see how they came out. I facetiously pointed out to my friends what a fascinating guy I'd become—tumbling stones. Took to lampooning myself as an ultra-suave character known as "Rock T."

By contrast, Lucien's idea of a good time in the Hamptons was to squirt a circle of lighter fluid around me in the pool and light it on fire. *No*, he didn't actually do that, but he joked about it often enough. He was a bit of a pyro. He particularly liked spraying lighter fluid on a lit barbecue, turning it into a towering inferno, which drove me crazy. He'd also mastered the crucial skill of one-handedly withdrawing a match from a matchbook and lighting it, all with a debonair flair. One weekend, he was reading a slim volume called *Smoking Is Sublime* and read snippets from it aloud. He was especially fond of a quote from Oscar Wilde: "A cigarette is the perfect type of pleasure. It is exquisite, and it leaves one unsatisfied. What more can one want?"

Matthew brought a watercolor set out to the house one weekend and before long had everyone trying their hand at painting. The thing was, you could just do it. It didn't require any particular talent or expertise like playing an instrument or writing a story. I don't think I'd painted since I was in grade school. Some afternoons, four or five of us might sit around the deck, each of us painting, some well, some poorly. It was engaging to try and mix the perfect blue, or let my mind go slack and see what abstract forms and images came out. Or attempt something representational and distort it half out of expressiveness, half out of ineptitude. It was best not to try too hard, to just give it a go. Occasionally, one of us would actually produce something halfway decent, and it might get displayed on the refrigerator door. I particularly enjoyed turning off the words-and-ideas part of my brain and becoming absorbed in the dozens of esthetic decisions—what color to use, how to mix it, what brush strokes to use, what more did the painting need, and so on. It was a relief, almost to the point of pleasure. Kind of like the way I imagine gardening. Or collecting seashards on a beach.

Those were fine summers.

January to October 1993.

Before I met Lucien, he was offhandedly described to me by my girlfriend, who hadn't yet met him herself, as sort of a male prostitute. Well, not exactly a male prostitute, she clarified, maybe more of a kept bisexual performer.

At the time, Sharon had recently met Lucien in the downtown club scene and excitedly told my girlfriend about this ultra-hip new guy she'd met, along with her somewhat confused impressions of him. He gave every sign of being into her as a woman, but he travelled in a mixed crowd, and people alluded to things that might have suggested she should steer away from becoming interested. But rather than being put off by the rumors of sordid behavior and sexual ambiguity, Sharon was impressed with his louche glamorous lifestyle and its chic-ness. Keep in mind, this was a young woman who sometimes worked as a dancer in a cage suspended over the swarming dance floor at Slimelight.

The specifics of the supposed decadence were that Lucien was involved in a hedonistic ménage a trois with Molly McFaghag, the aging blue-blooded fashion designer known for her perverse tastes and May-December liaisons, and her kept gay male companion, Lazaro, an exceptionally good-looking young Cuban guy. Molly and Lazaro were complete club habitués, and it seemed Lazaro served, among other things, as her social secretary, figuring out the right places to be on any given night, arranging transport, rounding up a tragically hip entourage, making sure the entrées went smoothly and the desired drugs were on hand.

Apparently, Molly McFaghag liked to watch, and there was speculation that Lazaro and Lucien performed for her in private. It was unclear whether the rumors included Molly receiving services directly. The conjecture included the possibility that remuneration was involved. This of course was highly juicy info, and my girlfriend eagerly shared it with me.

As I listened, an image formed in my mind of a lavishly appointed, dimly lit living room in a classic Park Avenue apartment with long hallways and scads of rooms. An elegant older woman in a long black evening gown reclined languidly on a sofa of silk brocade or maybe even a chaise lounge. X-ray thin, surgically maintained. Watching. Maybe smoking a cigarette in a long shiny black holder. (My imagination hammed it up.) And in front of her, on an intricately patterned, richly colored Persian carpet, the smooth naked bodies of two young men were entwined like Greek wrestlers.

It wasn't as if Sharon didn't get a bit unnerved by the gossip. But she assured my girlfriend that Lucien was being very hetero with her, and he seemed to be pulling away from Molly and Lazaro. Sharon probably figured she could maneuver the situation into a tamer version of hip decadence that would be palatable but still have some dark glamour. Also, she may have exaggerated things slightly for shock effect, or my girlfriend may have got things a bit twisted in translation.

For the first seven or eight months I knew Lucien, I assumed he was bisexual. I wasn't alone in my thinking. I mean, hey, on top of everything else, he'd gone to an English boarding school at one point. Outwardly, he was ambiguous, partly because of his dandyish style of dress, but he wasn't effeminate, more jaunty and rakish. He sometimes seemed to be deliberately confusing and amused by people trying to figure out what the situation was. As if he were toying with them.

How did I feel about my friend being bi-sexual? I'm fairly open-minded, but there are boundaries to my comfort zone. I do enjoy the amazing variety of weird and unique people in my city, many of whom wouldn't fit in any place else. Besides, I liked Lucien. And he was definitely shagging Sharon the sex kitten on a regular basis, to my vicarious pleasure. My girlfriend gave me some vague report about Lucien and Sharon having a scene with another couple—something involving blindfolds and bondage. I shrugged the whole bisexual thing off as not mattering one way or the other. He certainly wouldn't be my first friend who had gay experience.

One night, he and I went to an avant-garde play in an abandoned factory to see Matthew and others roll around naked on stage. I found the piece impenetrable. As Lucien and I were leaving, we bumped into Molly

McFaghag, Lazaro and another young man. Lucien introduced me. Molly actually wasn't that far from how I'd imagined her, though a bit more scary-looking. Lazaro was, as reported, extremely handsome in a suave another-era kind of way—Latin with light-brown hair, very feline. Lucien chatted with them for a few minutes, and the three of them glanced my way with seeming curiosity.

After we left, I asked Lucien straight out what the deal had been with him and them. He said nothing had ever happened although Molly and Lazaro had probably been angling for it. I told him how it had been originally presented to me, which made him laugh.

"But you've had gay experiences, right?" I asked.

"No." He shook his head.

"Oh, come on. It's no big deal. Of course you have."

"No," he said matter-of-factly.

"Not even once?"

"No."

I wasn't sure what to make of this. "You know," I said, "everybody thinks you're either bisexual or gay and pretending not to be."

He shrugged. "Yeah, I know. I don't mind. I'm comfortable with who I am. It's good to be…unclear sometimes. It gives you some mystery. And life can be more interesting when people don't have a clear grasp of who you are. This is a fascinating town, with all kinds of different people, lots of interesting scenes, lots of interesting people."

December 1994.

There was a time later on when Lucien and I were girlfriend-less, and we used to kid around about sharing a woman. Pulling a "Jules and Jim" as we put it. Inaccurately, since as he pointed out, the shared romance in the film wasn't particularly about pleasure-seeking. We even half-seriously speculated about a few candidates, though nothing much came of it beyond some lewd banter and a few young women rather confused at our joint flirtation.

I'd never shared a woman with another man. The activity clearly had gay overtones, no way around it. I mean, both men naked and aroused, having sex in front of one another, entering the same places, different places at the same time. Crossing swords, as the Frenchies say.

■ ■ ■

"He not busy being born is busy dying."

CHAPTER 7

April 1994. Downtown Manhattan.

Squeezebox again. The place was still delivering. The people who would've spoiled it didn't seem to have discovered it yet. The venue succeeded based on a specific social configuration: a lot of gay men, a good number of uninhibited straight women, and a smattering of straight guys, all happy to club together. It would've been easy for the balance to be thrown off, but the place was probably under a lot of people's radar, maybe because it was predominantly gay. Or maybe because it was so seedy, though New Yorkers do love to slum it.

We were our usual three. My girlfriend was absent as had become the norm. I probably should've focused on that a bit more.

I'd taken a weak hit of ecstasy, which was kicking in. Lucien wandered off, as he and Sharon each did regularly when they were out together, maintaining their independence. Sharon and I stood near the back wall in the main room. At the far end was a platform about a foot off the floor where the acts performed. A band was supposed to come on shortly, and the front two-thirds of the room was packed, but Sharon and I had space. We faced the stage, turned slightly toward one another. She was on my right, my left foot was up on a random chair. We weren't talking much, but it wasn't uncomfortable.

Things began to get hazy because of my altered state. Sharon started doing her dancing in place thing, which she could break into just about anywhere as long as there was music. The track pumping over the sound system was trance-techno with Middle Eastern accents, and she adopted a fitting style of flowing motion, particularly with her arms and hands.

She gradually angled herself more toward me, and her snaking hands passed in front of me, around waist level. I didn't think it was on purpose—not yet, at least— but she had my attention. Our eyes stayed directed toward the stage, though at least in my case without much focus. It was easy for both of us to act immersed in the darkness and the sonic cascade, not overly aware of the other.

Her weaving hands dipped lower and closer to the front of my black jeans. I didn't react outwardly but quickly got a raging hard-on. Then her hands began, for an instant here and there, to find that distance that isn't quite touching, but where you can feel the physical presence of the other person. The energy, the heat. And all the while, she kept her manner casual as if she were merely feeling the music. But she was having the effect I was sure she wanted—her specialty. I was throbbing almost to the point of faintness. Against my better judgment, I pushed my pelvis fractionally forward, straining to achieve the full-fledged contact I was dying for. But she was good, adept at her game. She maintained the infinitesimal space despite my shifting and leaning and her supposedly random undulation. As the band strolled on stage, she distinctly brushed the back of her hand up the length of my aching cock. My eyes rolled up under their fluttering lids.

She ended her performance, broke the spell. Oxygen flowed back into my brain.

April 1993.

When I was first getting to know Lucien and Sharon, my girlfriend and I had them over to my apartment for dinner along with Matthew and a few other friends. I remember early in the evening standing in the open kitchen with Sharon and my girlfriend, and Sharon flirting with me outrageously. Some of it was her automatically shifting into sex kitten mode. But in this instance, I was sure it was also because I was my girl-friend's *new* boyfriend, and Sharon had to show she could get a response out of me. I did respond inside, strongly, but focused intently on not letting it show.

My girlfriend took it all in. She'd even told me a few times previously that it was going to happen, not specifically that night, but sometime and probably with some regularity. She knew on some level she should be furious with Sharon, and did feel some animosity toward her, but on the whole she let it slide. They had a curious friendship. Among other elements, I think my girlfriend was one of the few people who largely bought into Sharon's "fabulous" act—at times, she seemed to actually think Sharon was a star—which was unfortunate in more ways than one.

As Sharon shimmied in my kitchen, she told me, as an indication of her intellectual proclivities, that as a child she liked to read the dictionary. ("Yeah," Matthew cracked later on. "How far did she get? Aardvark?" And he actually sort of liked Sharon, or at least got a kick out of her.)

During dinner, Sharon and I got into an argument. About six months before, Sinead O'Connor had appeared on *Saturday Night Live*, and at the end of her performance had held up a photo of the Pope and ripped it to pieces. The show being live, there was no opportunity to edit the incident out. She did it to protest the Catholic Church's stance on birth control and abortion, which was contributing to a lot of hardship in her home country, among others. In the ensuing public outcry, which the media eagerly joined in and egged on, it came out that Sinead had also recently refused at the last minute to perform a concert in New Jersey unless the venue agreed to break with their standard practice of playing "The Star Spangled Banner" before the show. You can imagine how that added to the uproar from certain quarters.

In any event, a couple of weeks after the *SNL* incident, there was a Bob Dylan tribute concert at Madison Square Garden, and Sinead was one of the many artists scheduled to perform. I went to the show. When Sinead came out on stage and started to sing her selection, large parts of the audience started to boo. She seemed puzzled as she sang the first several bars but then stiffened perceptibly and stopped. Stood there silently glaring at the crowd. The booing gradually died down, and there was a smattering of applause as pockets in the crowd expressed support for her. She signaled the backup band, led by a stone-faced G. E. Smith, and started the song again. The booing swelled up again loudly. About fifteen seconds in, she stopped abruptly, slashing her arm down toward the band. And stared icily out at the crowd for several long moments as the booing continued in uneven waves. She then stepped up to the mike and without any musical accompaniment shouted rapid-fire the lyrics to a Bob Marley song, which I later learned had an anti-censorship message. Then, to use a cliché, she stormed off the stage.

During the highly celebratory group encore (the show had been amazingly good), Sinead stood off to one side, separate from the dozens of other performers, and scowled at the crowd, and rather than sing in her normally exquisite voice, sang off-key, harshly against the grain.

Over coffee at the dinner party, a Dylan song came on the stereo, and Matthew started talking about what an enormous fan he was. I seconded his enthusiasm. "I went to the tribute concert at the Garden a while back. It was an unbelievably great show. The performances, the song interpretations, were amazing. I mean, Stevie Wonder doing *Blowing in the Wind*—brought down the house. Neil Young doing *All Along The Watchtower*, Chryssie Hind, *I Shall Be Released*. And The O'Jays, of all people, reinventing *Emotionally Yours*, making it their own soul/gospel anthem. And three female country singers absolutely killing it on *You Ain't Going Nowhere*. Mary Chapin, Rosanne Cash, and…and Shawn Colvin. Fantastic."

"I was there, too," Sharon said, surprising me and maybe others. Before I could ask how that had come about, she went on, "I think Sinead was great. Really courageous. The crowd was just a bunch of assholes."

"I don't know," I said. "I thought she handled the situation pretty badly. Foolishly. If she'd just kept singing, the booing would've died away and the moment would've passed. By stopping and confronting the crowd, trying to get them to back down, she turned the incident into way more than it had to be and sealed her fate in the process. When a crowd turns on you, it's like a wild animal. You're not gonna control it by force of will. If one person tries to take on an angry crowd in a battle of wills, the crowd's gonna win."

I didn't know if I completely believed what I said, but it had been my reaction at the show, and in any event it was what I came out with at the dinner.

"Well, I think it was bullshit the way the crowd reacted," Sharon said. "And I think Sinead was really brave to stand up for what she believed in."

Sharon may well have been right about this. But between her aggression and Sinead's holier-than-thou attitude, I couldn't help saying with a laugh. "Oh, come on. She was being an asshole." I admit it was abrasive of me.

"I mean, on top of everything," I went on, "she couldn't put her own ego aside and recognize the event was about paying tribute to Dylan. She recited the words to a Bob Marley song. And then she came out for the encore and stood separate from everyone else, focusing attention on herself and deliberately singing off key. She came off like a petulant child. And she seemed to relish the whole confrontation in a weird way. She was doing what she does—getting angry and making a scene."

Again, I wasn't sure if I fully believed everything I'd said. But it was just a dinner party conversation, and I tried to convey, in tone and manner, I was being a bit tongue-in-cheek, provocative for the sake of discussion. Maybe I wasn't clear enough or maybe I didn't try hard as hard as I should have. But I do know I didn't want a scene.

"Well, I think that's bullshit," Sharon said angrily. "I think there was a bunch of stupid pro-lifers in the crowd. And they were trying to censor somebody who was brave enough to stand up for her opinion."

"Well...," I said hesitantly.

"People like that are assholes," she continued. "I can't stand bullshit like that."

My sense was that if I continued the disagreement for one more round, she was going to make things very uncomfortable for everybody. So, I said, "Well, there you have it," with a contrived light laugh, and got up and went into the kitchen area.

Now that I think of it, Sinead and Sharon are not all that dissimilar. And, of course, I wasn't blameless, either.

Sharon and Dave-id. Oil and water.

July 1993.

Originally, I didn't want to have Sharon as a weekend guest in Wainscott. The question first came up shortly after my girlfriend and I got back from Majorca. My girlfriend wanted me to invite Sharon and Lucien out for a weekend, partly to reciprocate, partly to have some of her friends out there. I got the sense she'd already semi-extended the invitation. I was of course fine with Lucien coming, but Sharon had turned me off so much in Majorca that I didn't feel like dealing with her again for a whole weekend. And I thought some of my other guests would find her unpleasant to have around, too, though as it turned out I underestimated her entertainment value.

What would have been so bad? I mean, yeah, I didn't like her, but she'd be there as a guest for my girlfriend and Lucien, not me. So, why not?

Well, for one thing, she brought next to nothing to the table conversationally. For another, she wore a value system on her sleeve that strictly stayed on the surface, hard to take even for a person as shallow as me. And then there was her need to be the center of attention. She demanded it. If the focus didn't come around her way regularly—sometimes just a few minutes of non-attention was enough—she'd toss her hair or adjust her already short skirt so that more leg showed, or maybe stand up and stretch, or even dance around a little if music were playing. It was laughable how transparent she was. Or she might burst into the conversation going on around her with a brash opinion or shock-value remark that had next to nothing to do with what was being discussed.

Her worst social quality, though, by far, was how she dealt with disagreement. I mean, most people like being right, winning the argument, but it depends on how you go about it and how hard you push. When Sharon encountered disagreement, she essentially had two ways of dealing with it. The first was *baffle 'em with bullshit*. As soon as she found she was doing poorly in the rational back and forth, she'd get agitated and shoot off on some tangent with an irrelevant remark, or forcefully make some sweeping generalization. Or sometimes just launch into pure double-talk that made no sense at all.

If that didn't produce results, some yielding from the other side, she'd resort to her go-to move—threatening discord. Via tone of voice, confrontational manner, general nastiness. And if you didn't back off at that, she'd poison the air with a crackling of hostile energy, or maybe even make an out-and-out scene. And remember, I'm talking about social conversations with nothing in particular at stake. Sharon didn't get that.

She also used this last tactic in contexts other than conversation. For instance if my girlfriend wouldn't loan her some item of clothing or join her on some outing, she might implicitly threaten to withhold her friendship, such as it was, or actually withhold it. Maybe I shouldn't call it friendship. Maybe I should just call it her willingness to hang out with someone, to include the person in her fabulous social sphere, which is really what she had on offer.

Why did people put up with her? Well, people are young—for about twenty-five years at least—which explains a lot. And she was truly gorgeous and sexy. It may have been that simple—"that inconsequential, infinitely powerful creature: a pretty girl."

One evening in Majorca, a few days after the night she pranced around in her vintage platform shoes, our contingent wound up in a lovely town square in Pollensa, near the northern corner of the island. We settled down at an outdoor café and ordered a couple of pitchers of sangria. Unfortunately, Sharon and I almost immediately got into an argument about the existence of God, with me standing for atheism, of course. Now, I know this is a delicate topic, and I have friends who believe in God in one way or another. So, while I have my views on the subject, I don't usually push them hard. But Sharon had a way of bringing out the worst in me. Besides, every so often, the existence of a higher power is an interesting topic to tackle. Lucien's assemblage had coalesced during our days on the island into a cohesive group, and all sorts of interesting subjects were coming up in conversation. I guess I thought our gathering in the charming town square, with its stately old church in one corner, would be an okay context in which to have some dialectic about God.

How wrong I was. Sharon took me on in a big way. As she'd done in the Sinead argument, and to a lesser extent with Lucien in discussing *American Psycho* a few days before, she quickly asserted her viewpoint in a confrontational way. And threatened to spoil a very pleasant, almost idyllic occasion. Annoyed, I decided not to back off this time and locked horns with her to a point where some of the others shifted uncomfortably in their chairs, which was a shame because sitting there in that tranquil plaza in the soft light of dusk should have been a complete and utter pleasure.

Now, here I was back home being pressed to have Sharon out to Wainscott.

I eventually gave in because, all things considered, it was the right move. And it didn't turn out that badly.

By the time the next summer rolled around—the Istanbul summer—my friendship with Lucien was fully established, and I'd settled into being able to deal with Sharon in groups, so the two of them were regulars out there. Even after Lucien left for Europe in late July, Sharon kept coming out because of my girlfriend.

The two young ladies would lie on lounge chairs by the pool endlessly reading fashion magazines, talking about Christy, Claudia, Naomi, Calvin, Ralph, and Todd. They sunbathed topless, and Sharon had this disconcerting habit of absent-mindedly playing with her nipples, sometimes even when she was talking to you. You think I'm exaggerating, but I'm not. Sometimes, she played with her nipples when she was standing right in front of you, addressing you.

She could be a one-woman pageant and definitely

added spice to the occasions. The people gathered on any given weekend usually had a rollicking time. Especially dinners out on the deck under the stars. We had local corn roasted crispy brown at almost every dinner, grilled salmon, tuna, and lobster on the barbecue. Steak for Lucien as he'd picked up a nasty bug in Central America once and since then dastardly things happened to him when he ate seafood.

Like most English people, he liked his meat well-done. I argued that he was destroying all the flavor. He responded that the way he liked his meat prepared depended on the quality of the establishment he was in—in a dive, he had his steak well-done, in a decent place, medium, and in a top joint, medium rare. He added with elaborate emphasis that with an "idjit" like me picking the meat and manning the grill, he'd have his steak well-done.

Laughter, music, conversation. Out under the stars. Trees swaying in the breeze, rustling leaves. Me proclaiming with gluttonous tipsy pleasure that all I wanted to do was go upstairs and be alone with my lobster.

Withnail and I. What can I say? Watching the film is a quasi-religious experience for me.

I brought a copy out to Wainscott at the end of the summer of '93, Labor Day weekend. Some of the gang had seen it before, Lucien and I several times each. On a rainy afternoon, we sprawled out around the living room and pushed *Play*. The exquisitely sweet sounds of King Curtis on alto sax trilled over the opening shot of a messy-beyond-belief Camdentown flat—the best version ever of *A Whiter Shade of Pale* and instrumental at that.

It struck me during the viewing how much the film related to that time in my life. Not only is it about a rollicking trip to a country house, but it also captures a certain mad bacchanalian search for…for something elusive.

Camdentown, north London, Fall 1969. A couple of struggling out-of-work actors, both around thirty, close friends living together in the squalid abode, approaching the end of their rapidly waning young manhoods. One of them, Withnail (pronounced With-nul), is a dissolute aristocrat alienated from his family and their wealth. (His flatmate says to him, "If I were you, I'd ask my father for money"; his response: "If you were my father, you'd say no.") Withnail is an exceptionally entertaining but maddening personage. His flatmate, the "I" of the title (never referred to by name in the movie, but identified as Marwood in the screenplay) is quieter, less out of control, though still an essentially willing participant in the series of tragicomic escapades of which their lives consist. Not the star of the duo, but not as much of a lost cause either. The voice of reason as between the two of them to the extent there is one.

They each have begun to sense they're coming to the end of a certain stage of life without the foggiest notion of what they're going to do next. The kind of good times they've been having till then have begun to run out of steam, and the lads are getting a bit nervous.

The plot, to the extent there is one, is that in the midst of a highly varied drug and alcohol binge ("drifting into the arena of the unwell"), they decide they need to escape their louche unseemly lives and get away to the country for a few days. For some soul-cleansing. They persuade Withnail's gay uncle Monty to let them use his remote country cottage, at the unexpected price of Uncle Monty showing up and Marwood having to deal with his advances. Not much happens. Other than a continuous stream of hilariously profound moments. And in the end, there is a resolution of sorts.

Why did the movie speak to me so strongly? Some of it has to do with the genuine friendship between two highly appealing characters. And the bacchanalia, the road-trip/expedition element of it. The antic colorful dialogue alive with feeling. The gut-splitting humor. It's an extremely rich film. But the thing that ultimately makes it so special is its profoundly moving nature. It captures two spirited young men trying to find their way into full adulthood and yet fighting against it tooth and nail. On a quest for kicks, but also on a quest to come to terms with grown-up life and its realities. Trying to emerge from the morass of hedonistic young adulthood, the throes of libertine youth. The movie conveys, as poignantly as I can imagine, that period in a young man's life, and how it necessarily has to come to an end. The film is about the last gasp of glorious havoc-wreaking irresponsibility.

The crew that weekend particularly enjoyed Uncle Monty, who spins off one signature piece of melodramatic dialogue after another. At one point, he declares in his extraordinarily affected manner regarding the failed acting ambitions of his youth, "It is the most shattering experience of a young man's life when one morning he awakes and quite reasonably says to himself, I shall *never*…play the Dane."

■ ■ ■

"The dick dictates," Lucien used to say with a grin.

CHAPTER 8

That first night in Istanbul at 2019—remember, Mad Max goes to Constantinople—I was audience to a few small but intoxicating pieces of theater.

The first occurred around two in the morning when the night-space was at its delirious swirling peak. I stood on an elevated walkway, high on grass and ecstasy, leaning over the railing, watching the churning swarm of dancers below. The crunching techno-rhythms reverberated through my body as if the earth were shaking. Also, as mentioned earlier, I had the sensation of having been beamed from my regular life—constricted by work in the corporate world and missing a certain vitality—to a magical metropolis across the globe where I felt profoundly alive, close to exaltation.

Giles was standing a few feet to my right, also

leaning on the railing gazing down. We were both in our own worlds, Lucien and Azine off somewhere. Swirling below were people, faces, bizarre fashion statements.

On the right side of the dance floor, a woman emerged from the melee. One moment, there was a mass of swarming bodies, and the next there was a stunning woman dancing by herself in their midst. The dancers around her seemed to spontaneously give way, clearing space for her, which gradually increased until she was alone in a circle of revelers.

She was dressed in a red-and-white candy-striped bathing suit—one piece, 1950s style—glittery smoky-nude stockings, seams up the back, and sparkly black platform high heels. About six feet in her shoes, with a wild mane of curly brown hair and a staggering body—roller-coaster curves, corset-thin waist. She had coffee-colored skin and was exotic-looking, probably Turkish, but possibly Brazilian or Persian or of some other mocha-colored background.

Her face had thick sensual features made up to entice, and when they flashed my way across the airy space, my brain fogged up with whispered suggestions.

Whoever was handling the lighting began to feature her. It struck me that maybe she was working for the club or a promoter. Hip attractive people are often hired to just hang out and dance, enhance the crowd beyond the glamour of the performers sashaying around on raised platforms and the like. On the other hand, maybe it was just that the lighting guy knew a good thing when he saw it.

A driving electric piano rose out of the fuzzy bass-laden mix, and jungle sounds imbedded in the recording sprinkled the room. The dancer writhed sinuously, arms like serpents. Her movements were fluid as mercury, guided by pure instinct, not a tinge of thinking going into them. Power emanated from her, glistening in the air. She toyed with it, flexed it casually, offhandedly, seemingly for no reason other than to feel it. She was perfect, mind-boggling. No exaggeration. And I've seen a lot of women strut their stuff.

I watched her from my position for a half-hour or so, mesmerized, checking at one point to make sure Giles was taking it in as well. I needn't have been concerned. It was a sweet stinging pleasure just to watch her. As if she was giving off euphoria-inducing fumes wafting into everyone's brains. She was so out-and-out sexy, so poignantly erotic. She turned sensuousness into an art form. She spoke to the groin with authority. I was getting carried away in my private hyperbole. But hey, I was in the moment and didn't harness my free-wheeling thoughts.

Her beauty had a fantasic vulgarity. Not in any negative sense, though the word hardly has any other connotations. I mean vulgar in a wild primal sense, embracing the Pan within. There can be beauty in vulgarity, which most people don't get. They think vulgar is only disgusting, one of the ultimate dismissive words. What they don't understand, would probably even dispute, is that vulgarity can be closely related to sensuality, can be an expression of potent human desire and sensation deep within. Matters of the nether region.

I gazed at her sensuous face, her lush untamed hair, tantalizing attire. Her extravagant body, riveting undulation. She was a moving violation. Tuned in without the slightest shame to something as basic and powerful as it gets. Carnality. I had a flash of a gypsy woman in ancient times dancing barefoot around a blazing campfire, skirt and hair whirling, shadowy figures around her in the darkness watching. This woman was a performer. She pulled it off completely, and for that I privately bowed to her across the room. In thrall.

That's all that happened. It didn't even occur to me to try and meet her. She was from a different galaxy. And there was the likely language barrier. It wasn't about meeting her, anyway, trying to get anywhere. It was about the performance, the enchanting vision and savoring it. That's all I wanted. It was an ideal ingredient for my first night in Istanbul.

Wandering around on my own later, I sighted a pretty dark-haired girl dancing by herself on a slightly elevated area in front of the DJ booth. She was dressed simply—white T-shirt, black jeans, and delicate flat shoes. Understated, a vivid contrast to the entrancing siren from earlier. Her dancing consisted of one graceful move repeated again and again to the rhythm of the music. Restrained. Lit from above, her T-shirt snug, the swell of her pert breasts looked heavenly as she swayed.

Then, quite late, I watched a strangely familiar, male go-go dancer on top of one of the purgatory-like smokestacks at the far end of the room. He was tall and thin with short strawberry-blond hair, very effeminate. He moved smoothly with little effort and a studied nonchalance. Something in his manner gave the impression that he was glorying in his faux stardom up there on the pedestal high above the crowd. I fabricated a story in my head that he'd grown up in difficult straits yearning to be a star, any kind of star, but after various disappointments would eventually come to realize he didn't have the goods. And the scene I was watching was the closest he was ever going to get.

Somewhere in my reverie, I realized that visually—the hair, the lithe figure, the slouching glide— he reminded me of my nameless girlfriend back in New York.

"Doctor U.V.," Lucien exclaimed as Giles walked up to join us, "you've got to hear this." We were having late morning coffee at the Bebek Café, Islamic singing drifting over from the mosque next door, high and whiny but pleasant.

"No," I said with a laugh.

"Why not?" Lucien demanded as Giles sat down.

"Well, you know, it doesn't show me in the best light. And Giles just met me." It was our third morning in Istanbul.

"Oh, don't be stupid. He already knows you're a wanker. Come on, out with it."

Giles ordered Turkish tea from the old man waiting tables, yawned and stretched and then looked at me expectantly.

Guys regaling one another with sexual exploits can easily come off as distinctly uncool. It's one thing to bed a woman, it's another thing to talk about it. Or worse yet, boast. Telling others often has an adolescent quality and can be decidedly inelegant. It frequently glaringly reveals certain male qualities that are not the most attractive, especially from a woman's point of view. Such as striving to achieve promiscuity, divorcing sex from emotion, and the conquest often being the sole objective.

Bragging is especially unappealing. Success with women, like physical prowess and careers, is one of the basic areas of competition among guys. When a guy brags about his sexual exploits, it's like some macho jerk telling you how he kicked somebody's ass for no good reason, or some loser trying to impress you with how much money he makes. All of which are variations of a guy trying to show how big his dick is (a favorite expression in the music business).

On the other hand, chasing women and sex make for some interesting stories and shouldn't be completely off limits for guys shooting the breeze with one another. Such activities are a rich subject, full of flavor—weird, funny, electric, euphoric, sometimes sad, even pathetic, the whole range. Besides, guys can't be expected to live as if a basic part of their nature isn't in them.

There's a joke about a guy who gets shipwrecked on a desert island. One day, he sees another boat going down offshore but only manages to save one person—Claudia Schiffer. Naturally, she's incredibly grateful, and she says to him, "You saved my life. I can't thank you enough. How can I ever repay you? I'll do anything you want."

"Anything?" he says, incredulous.

"Well," she says hesitantly, "you saved my life, so yes, I guess anything."

So, for the next few weeks, he has her perform for him sexually in every way imaginable. Absolutely everything. Then one day, he says to her, "So, when you said you'd do anything, did you really mean it?"

She says, "Well, yes, I guess so."

"Okay, then will you pretend to be my friend Bob?"

She's a bit surprised and says, "Uh, after the past few weeks, I didn't think you were that way. But I did say I'd do anything, so if you want me to, yes."

She puts on a deep voice and assumes some male mannerisms and starts pretending to be his friend Bob.

And right away, the guy says, "Bob, you won't *believe* who I'm fucking!"

See, a guy's got to tell somebody.

Sitting there at the Bebek Café, I shrugged and plunged into my story. "I met this Russian woman a few months back. Right on the street in midtown, waiting on a corner to cross. She moved to New York a few years back and works as a hairdresser at some salon near there. I immediately picked up on a really strong sexual vibe coming off her. Her sexiness was really amped up, beyond just her appearance." I shook my head, remembering.

"She was sort of…Tartar-looking…you know, that Eurasian blend they have in southern Russia. Actually, just north of here, across the Black Sea. There's something very cool about that look for me. And she was a very pretty version of it.

"Sure enough, it turns out her main thing, overshadowing everything else, is being sexy. Pouty lips, short skirts, high heels, the whole deal. Tight little T-shirts showing off her great breasts, giving glimpses of midriff. It was her thing. She oozed sex." I stretched in my chair, arching my back harshly to get the kinks out.

"It's horrible to say, but she was almost completely vacuous. Hardly any smarts or interests, no knowledge of the world. She was like a blow-up doll, a perfect boy toy. Not in a sad or fucked up way, though. She was happy-go-lucky. She seemed perfectly okay with the world relating to her as a sexy young woman.

"Anyway, I was dying to sleep with her from the

moment I saw her. So, I take her out, and at the end of the evening, it becomes clear she's game. But I don't have any place to take her. I can't take her to my place because my girlfriend's got a key. And she won't let me come to her place because it seems she lives way uptown in some very humble place, and she's embarrassed. I was beyond frustrated."

"That's when you need a fuck pad," Lucien chimed in.

I acknowledged the truth in his crude remark with a look. "Anyway, I take her out again, and this time we're groping on the street. I'm bursting at the seams. We're in midtown and I suggest maybe going up to my office. It was late, around midnight, and there probably wouldn't be anybody up there. I'd told her I had a girlfriend, so she knew we couldn't go to my place. After a bit of hemming and hawing, she agrees. And then it was *on*.

"We get up to my office and start going at it. At one point, she has on just panties and high heels and stands up against one of the floor-to-ceiling windows, arms outstretched, looking at the city and all the lights. She looked crazy sexy, and I had this flash of seeing her like that from a helicopter hovering outside the window.

"The thing was, though, the building is one of those buildings where you can't turn out the ceiling lights. They're on twenty-four hours a day. Something to do with energy conservation, though that makes no sense to me. Anyway, with the lights on, the atmosphere, which already was a bit off—I mean, you can imagine, taking a girl up to your office the first time you're with her 'cause you've got a girlfriend—not exactly elegant. It was far from conducive to a maximum good time.

"But across the hall from my office is a conference room where you *can* turn out the lights. So, I take her in there and lock the door. We lay down on the carpet and go at it in the dark. It's fantastic. No harsh lights, just nice velvety darkness to lose yourself in. She decides she wants to get on the conference table, two big polished slabs of wood, twenty-five feet long. So, we get up there and take off whatever clothing we still had on. I'm inside her, on top, and all of a sudden I hear the crackling sound of a walkie-talkie out in the hallway—the sound of a security guard making his rounds. I freeze, mid-stroke. The walkie-talkie sound comes right up to the door, and the guard tries the handle. I'm lying naked on the conference table, half inside this woman, waiting for the guy to find his passkey and open the door. I'm hoping like hell he has instructions for dealing with situations like this, and they give him some discretion. I mean, situations like that have to come up every so often, and I'm hoping that being a senior executive counts for something." I shake my head, thinking back.

"Turns out I'm lucky. After checking that the door is locked, the guard just walks away."

"And the next day," Lucien added with a laugh, "Davey the Bull is walking past the conference room, and there's a meeting going on in there with a dozen people sitting around the table. And he sees a large stain right in the middle of the table."

I grinned sheepishly.

Giles chanted rhythmically, "Davey the Bull. Davey the Bull had himself a debotchka."

We sat there and laughed, went over bits of the story, alluded to a few other encounters. It was another beautiful sunny day on the Bosporus. I turned my coffee cup over to see the pattern formed by the grounds, not that I had the faintest idea how to read them.

Giles, inspired, I guess, said, "Let me tell you about Evie Cranston-Jones, the upper-class slut from hell."

Lucien had mentioned her in passing a few times, without elaboration. He and I grinned.

"William knew her first," Giles started out, referring to another friend of theirs back in England. "He used to stop by her place, not for out-and-out sex, but for… well…sexual favors. She was posh. Really posh. A total Sloane Ranger. Not the Laura Ashley variety, either. One of those upper-class party girls who's out of control, dances on tables and all that. Thinks she's entitled to behave however outrageously she wants, and that when *she* does it, it's not tacky or rude."

"Yeah, I know the type from when I lived there," I said.

"She was rail thin," he continued, "sleek blond hair, Vidal Sassoon style. And," he said with mock lasciviousness, "she was *dur-tee*. She liked to put it about." He shrugged and added matter-of-factly, "She really liked sex.

"Anyway, William invites me to come round with him one evening for a bit of the old double-bonk. And we're at her place hanging out, drinking wine, smoking hash. And at one point we just fronted it. You know, like, 'Evie, darling, it's your lucky night.' And she went for it.

"We go into her bedroom—really plush, all decked out with thick floor-length curtains, scarves and fabrics draped everywhere. Standing candlelabra, wax melted down all over it. We strip and get on the bed, Evie in the middle. We start making out with her and fondling. William and I are each sucking one of her tits. She stops us and gets out this enormous vibrating dildo from her night table. The thing was like a truncheon. But she can't get it to work. So, I take the thing apart while William is diddling her, and I reconnect the battery terminals or something. And it works! She's super pleased.

"She lays back and starts playing with herself and working the dildo in. Then she puts one of her heels at the bottom of the vibrator and guides it round and round and starts twirling her nipples with her fingers." Giles leaned back in his chair and made a show of demonstrating the act. Lucien and I laughed.

"William and I are on either side of her, wanking away, and she's working herself into a frenzy. She's completely concentrating, lost in her own world. And that's when we give her the old stereo seminal fanfare."

We laughed. It was funny. Yeah, we were being immature and crude and vulgar. But that was us. As Augie March said, "Better to give in and be yourself than live your life a stranger." Or something like that.

Oh, and let's not forget my debotchka story, which shows I cheat on my girlfriend, making me a lying piece of shit.

"Ee's a performer." Yet another of the lines Lucien appropriated from the film *Performance*. Said in reference to Chas, as in, *"Allo, Chas. 'Oo do you think you are?"*

Chas's job as a criminal was, among other things, to put the "frighteners" on people when necessary—"flash little twerps" as he referred to his victims in one scene. And when his fellow gangsters confront him about going renegade, one of them sardonically alludes to how good he is at his work, saying with a sneer, "Ee's a performer." Which leads to a line I always enjoyed, delivered in a quiet sinister way by the other villain. "Yeah, 'ee enjoys his work. And that ain't the 'alf of it."

Anyway, "Ee's a performer" (or "she's a performer") is a line you can use in any number of contexts. (Like "he's a closer.") Anytime a guy does something really well or produces a good result, you can convey that by saying, "He's a performer." Like when the front person of a band rivets your attention with their stage presence and charisma, completely aside from the music, as in, "Hey, man, that P.J. Harvey, she's a performer." Or when a woman is a genuine sack artist, you can say with meaning, "She's a performer."

Or you can just say it for the hell of it, for the sheer enjoyment of the phrase.

———————————————

Lucien told me another story once about Giles and William. William lived in London and had gotten involved with a black model named Giselle living in Paris. According to Lucien, she was "difficult but all right, African, dark with a body." She showed up in London once when William was out of town for one reason or another. Work may have unexpectedly required her to be there, or maybe she hadn't been clear with William when she was coming. In any event, he wasn't around, but Giles was. And he and Giselle got together and shagged.

William stopped seeing her a few months later, without having found out. But Giles felt extremely guilty, and the knowledge weighed on him heavily. A few months later, Wiiliam wrote Giles a letter and in one part said something like, "Why don't you deal with the past? Why don't you ever confront the truth?" Giles freaked out and called William right away and confessed, apologizing profusely.

It turned out William had been melodramatically referring to some other things from Giles' younger years and hadn't known anything about the betrayal. William was furious. He eventually got past it, though. He said she hadn't been important enough in his life for him to permanently lose a long-term close friend.

Lucien and women.

He and I were walking along the main street of Bebek one evening on our way to get the rental car from the dirt lot where we parked it. "You know, it's funny," I said, "you're such an ugly bastard, but beautiful women really do go for you."

He grinned and took a drag on his cigarette, shrugged and said, "Yeah, it's strange, though. Classically pretty women don't tend to go for me. You know, the uptown types or the full-fledged yuppies. It's usually only the downtown types that go for me, the ones with alternative tastes."

"Yeah, well, if you've got to have a limited audience, that's a good one to have."

We walked past a row of food shops—meat, fish, bread, cheese, desserts—a separate one for each, old school shopping.

"A lot of beautiful women don't like to be with really handsome guys," he said. "Sometimes it has to do with the fact they're beautiful themselves, and don't want to be with a guy who takes attention away from them that way. They don't want to compete with a man in their own strong suit. Besides, they're already bringing a healthy dose of good looks to the table and don't necessarily need a really great-looking guy to feed their heads, not if they're confident. For women like that, it's more of a statement to be with an intriguing-looking guy, a guy who gives off a certain something. And then, for some women, there's something unmanly about a guy who's too good-looking."

Lucien was far from ugly, but his handsomeness wasn't conventional. It took someone who liked interesting faces to fully appreciate him. There were plenty who did.

He looked cool. I can't describe it in any other way, beyond using that highly subjective, hard-to-define word. He just looked cool.

One night when it was only Lucien, Azine and me out for dinner, I particularly delighted in Azine's company for some reason, flirting with her within the bounds of how you're allowed to flirt with your friend's woman. Lucien was sitting right there. He was very secure in that way. This actually had become a curious part of our friendship—him bringing beautiful women into our orbit and me flirting with them. What was that about? Was it connected to me being so strongly drawn to him? I definitely got to flirt with some extremely pretty women I wouldn't have otherwise. I enjoyed it. I can be a fun flirt, if I do say so myself.

The women seemed to enjoy it, too, though I'm not sure they always knew what to make of the two of us. It was usually clear they were there for him. So, they must have wondered why I was I flirting with them. And why didn't he seem to care?

I do have an appeal that plays well to some women. And some women maybe found me more appealing because I was friends with Lucien.

Some of the women we dallied with were puzzled by our friendship. They couldn't quite put us together—the age difference, different types and all that. I enjoyed their mild confusion. Also, Lucien wasn't the easiest guy to flirt with. He held back. I think sometimes for the women, flirting with me was a way of flirting with him. All in all, the dynamic with women and the two of us got pretty blurry sometimes.

Lucien took it all in, amused, entertained. We complemented each other well. Partners in our escapades.

After Istanbul, at a time when Lucien was single, he became briefly involved with a beautiful young woman from Italy temporarily living in New York—Pa-TREET-see-ah. She was very sweet and fell head over heels in love with him right away in the extra intense way that young women can.

After an early love-making session, she exclaimed to him, "Fan-TAS-ti-co," which he found delightful.

As usual, I enjoyed flirting with her. And one night over dinner at Raoul's, I said to her, as he sat there listening, "Pa-TREET-see-ah, forget about this guy. You're too good for him. I'm the one for you."

Later on, when it became clear he didn't reciprocate her intense feelings, she sadly announced to him with her strong Italian accent, "Lucien, I *lahv* you, and you don't even care about me."

Then there was the time when Lucien and a hardcore fashionista woman he ran across all the time did the "big flirt", as he called it—the dance of possible romantic interest. You know, where both people make a lot of overtures, but neither goes out on a limb. As Lucien said, the big flirt can only go on for so long—either it becomes something more or runs out of steam. Anyway, Lucien, Matthew and I were having dinner one night in the East Village, and Lucien was meeting the fashionista woman afterward at the Tenth Street Lounge. He seemed preoccupied, and after he left, Matthew commented he must really like her.

I said, without really thinking, "No, he's just intrigued by her. I don't think he really likes any of them. Not in any meaningful way." As I said it, though, I knew I was wrong. He may not have been strongly drawn to any of the women I knew him with, other than Azine, but he liked all of them to some degree. He cared about Pa-TREET-see-ah, notwithstanding her woeful lament. He even liked Sharon, for all her glaring flaws and bullshit, which of course I couldn't grasp.

That was a key difference between him and me. He wasn't with women he didn't like. And I was, with some regularity. How did I feel about that? I suppose I had a measure of self-disdain due to this, but I accepted it. Back then, I was okay being with women I didn't like, for short periods at least. I will say, though, as the years have gone by, I've gotten less okay with it.

Over drinks one night, Azine amused me with a story of a strange man a friend of hers had met on the street in Manhattan. She, Lucien and I were sitting having cocktails on an elegant open-air terrace carved out of rock, high up a hillside overlooking the bejeweled bridges, glowing domes and minarets, the dark glistening waterway. The bar was called Sesame (as in *Ali Baba and the Forty Thieves*).

It was the night Giles stayed in. He'd told Lucien he had some things he wanted to think about, an obvious reference to the child his girlfriend was planning on bringing into his twenty-six-year-old life. When Lucien and Azine came over without him to pick me up at my hotel, I phoned Giles at Azine's apartment to try to convince him to change his mind. After all, we were in Byzantium and the night was young. It didn't seem like he should stay in by himself immersed in somber thought. There certainly were times for things like that, but this didn't seem like one of them. I had no luck, though. He let me know, appreciatively but firmly, that he really wanted to be by himself. I didn't press it but signed off echoing something Matthew had recently quoted to me from a

Jeanette Winterson book: "Remember, the cities of the interior are vast and do not lie on any map."

On the way to the lofty lounge hewn out of stone, Lucien said, "Giles sometimes tries to do the right thing for all the wrong reasons."

Azine's story of the strange man. When she was living in New York, a girlfriend of hers—a Turkish lesbian actress—was walking on West 72nd Street one morning when she was politely accosted by a homely overweight guy. Azine wasn't two or three sentences into the story when I guessed the guy's name—Robert Hogarth. I knew two other women he'd tried to pick up on the Upper West Side in the same way, and had heard of a third.

This guy had been prowling the neighborhood for years, trying to pick up attractive women. The thing was he actually had a meaningful calling card of sorts, unlike most guys trying to pull off something like that. He had directed a feature film with Isabella Rossellini in it, something to do with terrorists in Paris.

From what I understood, he'd walk up to a pretty young woman on the street and say, "Excuse me, my name is Robert Hogarth, and I'm a film director. I noticed you and think you have a very special quality. Are you an actress by any chance?" I gather he wasn't remotely good-looking and came off a bit of weird. But you bet your ass, in the great city of New York, the hotbed of the actress/waitress, the Mecca of people who want to "make it", there were some women who stopped and gave him the time of day. Cautiously perhaps, but they'd talk to him, and as I said, he had some real credentials. Inevitably, some of the women fell for his pitch and hung out with him to one degree or another. Who knows what he managed to pull off, especially with the head cases running around New York. They're out there, and some of them are quite attractive.

As a foreigner, Azine's friend was maybe less able to read the social cues in NYC and possibly more open to oddballs. She also had the ego of an actress, often a peculiar combination of self-absorption and insecurity. In any event, she bought into Hogarth's sales job and actually got to know him a bit. She had coffee with him that day and got together with him a number of times afterward. She referred to him as Robert, which struck me as strange for some reason. Maybe it was that he was such a creepy-sounding guy, and calling him by his given name seemed like calling Jeffrey Dahmer "Jeffrey".

On one get-together, they were drinking wine in a cafe, and he told her about an exceptionally vivid epiphany he'd once had. He'd been in Marbella one summer for vacation and was staying in one of the highrise hotels that crowded the coast. Each room had its own balcony, and his was high up facing the sea. One night, he came in late from carousing, tired but wound up from the evening. He undressed and went out onto the balcony naked in the warm night air. The moon was full and he stood looking out at the Mediterranean. I picture him with a hairy belly bulging over the railing.

He gazed up at the moon and out at the massive shining sea. And on impulse, he began to masturbate. When he came, "thunderously" according to him, off the balcony into the night, an epiphany came to him that that was how the universe had been created. Up in the heavens, God had pleasured himself. And his volcanic ejaculation into the dark nothingness that was everywhere back then consisted of an enormous spray of planets and stars that became the universe. And according to Hogarth, that's why they call it the Big Bang.

Azine told the story delightfully, her laughter at the end sounding like a cluster of ringing bells.

It struck me that Hogarth was a prime candidate for the *Coffee Table Book*.

■ ■ ■

"I've got whores in my head. Whores in my head."

CHAPTER 9

Mid-July 1994. Wainscott.

We cruised out the boring L.I.E. in a rental car on our way to the summer house. I drove, Sharon was in the passenger seat, and Lucien was sprawled in the back, having recently woken from a nap. It was early Thursday evening, a couple of weeks before Lucien was to head off to Europe for the rest of the summer. We were getting an early start on the weekend. Other guests, including my girlfriend and Matthew, would be coming out the next evening. The three of us in the car had something special planned for Friday during the day, before the others arrived.

As we drove, Sharon told me about her and Lucien recently going to visit her friend, Heather, in Brooklyn. I hadn't met Heather but had heard a fair amount about her. Sharon knew her because they were both from St. Louis, though they hadn't known each other there. They were put in touch when they both moved to New York to go to F.I.T. at the same time. They became fast friends and hung out together constantly during their first semester. After that, though, they drifted in different directions. Heather dropped out of school before the end of her first year, but they stayed in touch. Now, it was a couple of years on; I think Sharon was between her junior and senior years.

Apparently, Heather was sexy in some obvious ways, and during her freshman year, she started stripping to make extra cash. A lot of extra cash. And before long, she got herself a mob-connected married boyfriend and a new pair of tits paid for by him. Currently, the boyfriend was in prison for a stretch, and she was living in Bensonhurst in an apartment he was paying for, driving around in a new Jeep Cherokee he'd bought for her, and occasionally getting screaming phone calls from the wife. Heather was off the pole, as they say, but I gathered she occasionally stepped out on her incarcerated sugar daddy.

Sharon had stayed in touch with her throughout all this because, according to Sharon, Heather was "underneath it all a sweet girl." I couldn't help but feel that part of their lingering connection was that Sharon wasn't all that different from Heather. She just had her sights set on a higher socio-economic path.

Sharon described the recent visit as social, but I suspected it had something to do with getting drugs, maybe ecstasy. She talked about Heather's current life, making it sound a bit cheesy but essentially pleasant. Lucien chimed in bluntly that Heather was "living the full-blown guido life." And then threw in, "It's a shame about her drug problem." He seemed to be picking up on an earlier conversation between them, and it sounded like he was kidding.

Sharon responded testily, addressing me more than him. "Heather doesn't have a drug problem. That's the amazing thing about her 'cause she's surrounded by drugs all the time. Her boyfriend's involved in dealing at a really high level. I've been at her apartment with a mountain of cocaine on the coffee table, and she wasn't interested at all."

Lucien let this little flurry pass, and then a minute or so later when Sharon was still talking about Heather, said off-handedly, "Yeah, nice girl. But it's a shame about her drug problem."

I didn't know what the background was, but it was clear he was goading her and wasn't serious. She rose to the bait, though, and went on a lengthy angry diatribe about Heather's troubled life and how she'd done so well to avoid a drug problem, though I don't think anybody in the car actually thought she had one. I wasn't sure what was going on, but it was obvious Sharon wanted Lucien to stop.

Lucien let her finish, watched an exit go by, then said casually, "Yeah, I know what you're saying, but you know, it *is* a shame about her drug problem."

I almost started laughing. I mean, it was obvious he was only saying it to provoke her. But she got furious anyway. I thought she was going to explode with anger, but it belatedly seemed to sink in that he was baiting her and there was no point in responding. She subsided into a sulk, and when I made my usual stop at the gas station at exit 70, she stormed off to the restroom.

Lucien and I stood outside the car stretching, and watched her walk away. He said to me with a mischievous grin, "Well, I've got my theme for the weekend."

I laughed. A good long belly laugh, fading away a few times and bubbling up again. I mean, yeah, it wasn't nice to provoke her, but it was funny to watch her try to control him through force of will while he pushed her buttons. She really didn't get him.

Who knows what goes on in the dynamic of any romantic couple?

———————————

There's a jargon in the record business, like most businesses, a way of talking, ever evolving. My epitaph-writing friend ("They'll put it on your gravestone—He Was A Closer."), when he was new to the industry, said he knew for sure he was in the record business when a product manager he barely knew left his office after a meeting and said, "Who loves you, babe?" And then there was the promo guy who liked to sign off his phone calls, "Rockin'." Not "bye" or "take it easy." "Rockin'." I remember the first time he said it to me. I sat afterward at my desk staring at the receiver in my hand, thinking, *Did he really say that?*

Earlier, I mentioned the term "juice." Bargaining power, as in, "He's got the juice" or "He doesn't have the juice." It must have been derived from the slang for electricity, which in turn was based on the sweet energy-giving fluids of fruit. Slang derived from slang.

In the 90s, a new way of using the word "get" came into vogue in the record business, as in, "I'm gonna be in LA next week, and I'll get with Benny." The word "together" was dropped and saying something as normal as "meet" wasn't hip enough. Record industry types *get* with people.

Then, the hip expression became "reach out," as in, "I'll reach out to Rocco." Meaning basically you were going to call him. There was a suggestion that the call was going to be for a favor or have some other overture-like quality, but essentially it meant to call somebody on the phone. But they couldn't just say that.

There was a guy I worked for—Bobby DiStefano, president of one of Apex's record labels. He was extremely accomplished at intimidation and regularly an asshole, though not much more than most players in the industry. The company got good results under his watch. One could say he was a performer.

Sometime after I started working with him, Bobby glommed onto a new expression he really loved. It resonated for him in every ounce of his being. For a while, he said it every chance he got, beat it to death. He loved to thunder it, with as much power and anger as he could muster. It made him feel good, you could tell.

One of his minions would inform him that, say, an artist manager wanted some concession (often money) or wouldn't agree to something we wanted, and if Bobby was inclined to challenge this, usually his knee-jerk reaction, he'd swell up and roar, "You tell him he can suck my dick!"

He loved saying it. He got such obvious pleasure, almost literally erupting with anger and power. It was fun to watch. A few times, I even reported things to him in a way to prompt him to say it.

Anyway, I arrived in Wainscott with friends one Friday evening, after a particularly explosive session with Bobby that afternoon, and over a dinner of linguini with homemade pesto, salad, and wine, I regaled my guests with Bobby DiStefano stories, topping it off by rising from my chair and bellowing, "You tell him he can suck my dick!"

My friends thought this was hilarious, which I suppose it was, even if not always in the immediate experience. Matthew joked that somebody should secretly tape Bobby yelling the phrase, then get some hard-core rapper to sample it. "I can just hear it," he said.

"A crunching beat with a vocal over it going, 'You tell him…You tell him…You tell him he can suck my dick.' It's got rhythm."

For the rest of the weekend, the more juvenile guys in our crowd responded to requests or remarks by yelling things like, "Hey, you can suck my dick." We even drunkenly howled the expression at the moon late one night. Boys will indeed be boys.

———————————————

Friday morning after the Heather car ride, the three of us gradually got up and congregated in the kitchen— Lucien, Sharon and I. I weighed out three doses of mushrooms on a scale I'd brought—7/8 of a gram for Lucien and I, 6/8 for her—threw them in the blender with some orange juice. We each drank the foul concoction, then settled down on the outside deck by the pool as the sun cleared the trees.

It was a spectacular day—cloudless azure sky, temperature on its way to the low 80s. In the clearing surrounded by trees and open to the sky, there was an idyllic sense of peace and privacy. The day had that wonderful quiet feel the South Fork can have on a weekday, a hint of what it must have been like back in the Jackson Pollack days when it was really the country. We relaxed, waiting, mildly nervous. It was the first time in several years that I'd tripped. There was a decent stereo in the house, and we moved it so the speakers faced out the sliding screen doors. I had a bunch of mix tapes with me. I leisurely rolled a joint—patiently shredded the fuzzy green and orange buds, laid out the right amount in the crease in such a way it would draw well. Then put it aside for later when rolling would be too complicated a task.

Pretty soon, with our otherwise empty stomachs, our systems began to wobble and drift. The waves came rolling in. Lifting, surging. Our systems roared. We took off for the ride.

It was nice. Really nice. It was just so beautiful in our little glen; the sun felt so good. I perceived our glade as especially safe and secure, a "fine and private place" where you could completely let go and forget all the strictures and pressures, annoyances, of regular life. It was fantastically relieving. During the early stages, we listened to Seal, whose music is sometimes too lush and syrupy, but that morning was ideal—atmospheric, layered, rhythmic, and of course the velvet voice wrapping itself around us like a sarong in the tropics.

I lit the joint and drew deeply a couple of times. I had a distinct sense of the sticky sweet resin melting into smoke, swirling into my lungs and sending THC into my rippling system to blend with the psilocybin. The booster rockets kicked in, and I was gone. *Zooming.* The rushes came on, oh, so sweet. Waves of pleasure in amounts never experienced by those who haven't indulged. The familiar apprehension that I was going to get too high arrived, but I felt too good to stay worried.

We spread out to different parts of the deck, each in our own world, making the loss of control, the dazed feeling, more comfortable, more okay. We were like children. I remember slowly walking around my area, enjoying the feeling of the soles of my feet against the sun-warmed grainy wood of the deck. I stayed close to the speakers, thirsting for volume. Sharon was on the other side of the pool, Lucien at the far end.

Sharon became fascinated with some leaves hanging from a branch over the railing. She wore only a bikini bottom, her pert little breasts on display along with the perky nipples she sometimes absent-mindedly played with. Her nymph-like body was a delight to gaze on, as always. Lucien and I wore baggy swimsuits. I was vaguely conscious, as maybe was he, that it would screw things up if a sexual vibe entered our atmosphere. The situation was very sensual though. We were pretty much unclothed, especially Sharon, and supremely immersed in bliss. The warmth of the sun, the aquamarine pool, refreshing water, nature all around us, drugs floating inside, heightened sense of touch and feel, the music inducing physical pleasure. Hedonism flowed in full force.

I lowered myself into the shallow end of the pool and climbed onto a big bright-pink inflated scallop shell, and sprawled on my back. The sun soaked into me, water lapped at my hands and feet. I felt as if I'd returned to the womb and was floating in amniotic fluid.

My girlfriend once gave Lucien a birthday card with a big yellow sun-face on it and told him that when she saw the card in the store, it reminded her of him.

Lucien, for some reason, decided he wanted to see what things looked like from underwater in the pool. We didn't have a facemask, so first he simply tried going underwater and opening his eyes. No success. He then tried putting his wrap-around sunglasses on and pressing them tightly against his face as he ducked under. Still no success. In the course of this, he managed to explain that what he wanted to experience was the visual of looking up through the water at the bright lush outdoors with all the colors and light refracted. He was sure this would be superb. Sharon and I watched and laughed, still half in our own worlds. He went inside and came out with some tape, proceeded to tape his sunglasses to his face in what he hoped was a watertight way. Failure once again.

If you've ever done psychedelic drugs enjoyably, you know they can have a highly liberating effect on laughter. It comes bubbling up from inside you where it seems to have been in storage for far too long, and gushes forth easily and spontaneously. You can easily get to a point where you're howling uncontrollably without anything funny having been said or done. It feels fantastically good, a total release, making you feel like you don't laugh anywhere near enough in regular life, or deep enough. The laughter wells up inside you and comes in waves and waves of rapturous internal massage. Sharon and I were beginning to get to that point watching Lucien. There was no choice in the matter, not that we found it objectionable.

He went back in the house and came out with a large clear plastic bag, which sent me into another round of mirth. He taped his wraparound sunglasses on again and started to put the plastic bag over his head.

"Hold on," I said, trying to catch my breath. "We're doing mushrooms, and you're about to put a plastic bag over your head and go underwater. We should think about this for a minute."

The two of them made an effort to sober up enough to consider this, and Lucien assured us he had his wits about him sufficiently. He put the plastic bag over his head, clutched it around his neck, and plunged. He came back up in about five seconds, claiming he'd had three seconds of clear prism-like vision, and it had been like a big stained glass window in a church.

"What I really need, though, is a mask," he concluded, which sent me into peals of laughter again.

Later, I remember dancing wildly by myself to the long grinding electric guitar lead in Neil Young's "Like a Hurricane," feeling like an epileptic marionette yanked on strings by the master. My "Pan within" was released

149

completely, ran free. Across the pool, Sharon quivered with giddiness. A hint of fear flitted across her face for a moment but was just as quickly replaced by a look of contentment. I stared for I don't know how long at the tops of some distant trees swaying like enormous pendulums in the wind from the ocean.

Lucien got another bright idea. He wanted to experience the taste of marshmallows with peanut butter while tripping. We'd purchased both items the night before along with the rest of the food for the weekend. I was sure this was a bad idea and told him so flat out. He was insistent, though. Sharon and I followed him into the kitchen, and I said, "Are you sure you want to do this? I mean, any food while you're peaking on mushrooms is a bad idea, but peanut butter and marshmallows? You're out of your mind."

He persevered, smearing peanut butter all over a puffy white marshmallow, and popping it into his mouth. He began to chew as we giggled and watched his face for signs of reaction. He chewed. And chewed. I cracked up so hard I was gasping for breath. He refused to give up, masticating away. He later said he got to a point where he didn't know whether he was chewing the marshmallow or the inside of his cheek. His face gradually took on a look of dismay, and I convulsed with glee. He finally gave up and deposited the remains in the wastebasket. And pronounced with disappointment, "That was *not* a good idea."

Lucien and I were hanging out in his apartment one evening before we went out. A mix tape of his was playing on the stereo, and a Tanita Tikaram song came on I'd never heard before. I liked it immediately. I'd thought I knew all her many gems. It had a rousing melodic refrain: "Sun-face, sun-face…" I got a copy for myself and whenever I heard it, Lucien's smiling face would materialize before my mind's eye.

Back out on the deck, we settled into our bacchanalia and sonic-bathing. Then all of a sudden the music stopped right in the middle of some hilarity of ours. We wandered over to the stereo like stunned children, but couldn't get it going again. I made an extra effort to focus, thinking how frustrating and incomplete the rest of the day would be without tunes. We managed to determine the stereo wasn't working at all—no lights, nothing. Then we discovered the lights in the house weren't working either.

Did this have something to do with how fucked up we were? Was there an obvious solution we were missing? Was it something we'd done? Were we even perceiving the situation correctly? Shit, the refrigerator wasn't working. And we had a weekend's worth of food in there and other guests arriving that evening expecting dinner. You can't really function in a country house without a refrigerator. Shit! Lucien tried the phone and it didn't work. We were in the goddamn *Twilight Zone*.

We were still flying. And totally flummoxed. Lucien and I struggled to pull it together, to focus, but Sharon started to cackle uncontrollably. I wished she would stop, but she didn't. The thought of a fuse box loomed confusingly in my brain. We went outside and looked through the woods at the few other houses you could see partly through the trees, scanned them for signs of electricity or distress. No indication either way. I started to walk through the woods to the nearest house, but stopped myself, thinking maybe it wasn't such a good idea. I was far from confident I could avoid coming off as highly disoriented in any interaction with neighbors, if they were even in residence. And I had a vision of myself wandering off and becoming completely absorbed with some fungus on a log, forgetting what I was supposed to be doing.

Back in the house, Sharon totally lost control. She simply could not stop shrieking hysterically with laughter.

"Lucien, come on," I said. "We've got to focus. Figure this out. Concentrate! We're on mushrooms. Do you think it's just our house? What could be causing it?"

Lucien struggled to collect himself. Sharon continued cackling. He tried the phone again. It worked! Nothing else, though. Partial relief at least. In short order, a helpful telephone operator led us to the local electric company and fantastic news—it wasn't just our house; it was an area-wide problem and would be fixed within a half hour.

We were massively relieved. We relaxed and chuckled at a normal level, the good feeling seeping back in. I couldn't believe it. The one day we decided to do mushrooms, the first time in years for me, and there was an area-wide power outage in the middle of it. I'd thought I was going to lose it. We straggled back outside, and suddenly the music came back on. Happiness. Our journey resumed.

A little while later, I said, "Hey, how about the beach?"

Lucien and Sharon looked at me, considering. I could see them thinking, *Would we like it there? What if we didn't?* The idea seemed to have some appeal.

"How would we get there?" Lucien asked. It was a short drive or a fifteen-minute walk.

"We'll drive," I said brightly.

"*Can* you drive?" asked Lucien. He'd lost his own license a few years back in England—something to do with the "fiercest hassle ever" coming on the radio and inspiring him to a rash degree of acceleration.

"Yeah." I nodded, trying to reassure them. "I'll drive really slow. It's not far, and it's all back roads, no traffic."

We threw towels and a big bottle of water into the car, grabbed some tapes. And we were off to see the Wizard. I turned the car around so we were facing the long driveway through the woods and paused there for a few moments in our sanctuary-like clearing.

"You sure you can do this?" Lucien asked.

"Yes," I said, feeling spacey. I put the car in drive and we started to move forward very slowly. The driveway, as mentioned earlier, was a serpentine dirt road, about a football field long, through trees that created a thick leafy canopy overhead. On mushrooms, there was something magical about plunging into this tunnel of foliage, sunbeams sprinkling all around. We cruised slowly through the glowing cloister-like grove, the car rocking gently in the sandy tracks. Sharon said something to the effect that the look on my face was that of a totally happy child, and I must say my receptors were wide open. About halfway to the road, I unfortunately became absorbed in the intricate beauty of a particular tree, and Lucien had to shout "Hey!" to keep me from cheerfully driving into it. Out on the road, my admiration for a particularly statuesque stand of towering elms almost caused me to go straight at a T-junction rather than taking the necessary right, and Lucien had to sharply say "Hey!" again.

I've always loved trees. They can have exceptional beauty, different than any other kind. Trees and elephants. They have deep echo-filled resonance. When I was a kid, the Ents, the gigantic walking trees of Middle Earth, captured my imagination completely.

———————————

Lucien was an enchanter. If he took a liking to you, he drew you in and spun his charm. He seduced. Not in a sexual way, though for a few women there was that too, of course. And people almost always responded. It was easy for him. It was his nature.

———————————————

The beach was sublime. It's wide and goes on as far as you can see, both east and west. That afternoon, it was fairly empty, a couple of mothers with kids, some walkers, one with a dog running in and out of the water. It was late afternoon, the light pristine. We wandered a little way along the shoreline. It was then that Lucien wrote the "Allo, Chas…" quote in enormous letters in the wet sand. Sharon found a crab claw with vivid purple, orange and pink coloring, and thought it was the most beautiful thing she'd ever seen. I decided to try the ocean, though dipping a foot in the water told me the water temperature was bracing, and the surf looked rough.

Leaving Lucien and Sharon on the beach, I walked in, getting used to the chill, feeling how strong the undertow was, trying to get a sense of whether my 'shrooming self could handle this sea. The first row of white-capped waves didn't start until about twenty-five-yards out, and there were six or seven rows beyond, indicating a submerged sandbar. I got myself out to about the fourth row of rollers, more than waist-deep on the sandbar, and they were hitting me pretty hard. I stayed there awhile, thinking maybe I shouldn't push it. The coldness of the water didn't bother me; it was invigorating. I enjoyed the sensation of the waves crashing into me, the water surging and swirling around me. Bare-chested to the saturated blue afternoon sky, the dark sea spread out before me, my body rocked back and forth, spray hit my skin. I watched row after row of big noisy breakers come pounding in. Mesmerized. There was a majesty to the gargantuan natural dome above me. I would have seen it that way even without the hallucinogen, but the splendor of the scene came over me more easily with the drug. It was cathedral-esque.

I gradually grew more confident and went in deeper, where the waves loomed really large. I had to plant myself and lean far into them to keep my footing. I didn't want to go so far out that I couldn't touch bottom, given my condition and the power of the sea. I wasn't entirely sure I'd be able to get back in safely. A few times in the past, I'd underestimated the power of the sea. These waves were serious. But exceedingly cool as well. It became a challenge to keep my feet, keep my head above water. I made a game of it, leaning further and further into the roaring walls of water, pushing my limit, daring the sea to get me, sweep me off my feet, engulf my still semi-dry head. Powerful currents pushed and pulled at my legs, sucked me off balance. The depth fluctuated wildly. Massive white-topped swells smashed into me. I was King Canute commanding the sea to go back.

Don't ask me why, but for some bizarre reason, as

I was struggling to maintain my footing, the thought of Bobby "Suck My Dick" DiStefano popped into my psychedelicized mind. I had an addled revelation that disagreeing with him was like walking into an enormous wave. I pictured him sitting across from me at his round marble conference table, and remembered the few times I had directly disagreed with him and encountered his extreme displeasure. I envisioned him swelling up, almost literally rising from his chair, and blasting me with a tremendous roar. It was like walking into an enormous wave. As I struggled to stay upright, keep my head above water, I thought, *That's what corporate life is like. You can only walk into the waves for so long, and if you keep doing it, sooner or later they're going to sweep you away.* And that was when a big one crashed over me, sending me tumbling back toward the shore.

I pulled my legs out of the suck of the undertow and stumbled out onto the slope of wet sand. I felt grand. Alive.

That evening before the others arrived, the three of us had come down most of the way, though objects still had halos for me. We were about to take showers and ready ourselves to deal with people in a normal state of mind. Lucien and I stood in the dining room chatting, and I said with a smile, "Hey, that was a great day. Really great. Thanks for…I don't know…" I shrugged and went to give him a hug. For an instant, he seemed flustered, unsure of my intent. But I guess he quickly sensed it was a gesture of affection, closeness, and we briefly embraced.

———————————

A few days later, I received a fax at work that read:

> *To: David Burdon*
> *Re: Eating Your Words*
>
> *Candiru fish—a member of the Trichomycue-ridae group…Mammals including humans have had their urethra (Jap's eye to an igno-ramus like you) penetrated by the Candiru, which is known to swim up the flow of urine mistaking it for the expulsion of water from the gills of larger fish.?*
>
> *With smug self-satisfaction, Lucien*

■ ■ ■

"Remember," his smoky voice whispered, "nobody knows where you are."

CHAPTER 10

April 1995. Downtown Manhattan.

Squeezebox. The three of us had been going there a lot—Lucien, Sharon and I. Late that night, we were lounging downstairs in the basement room. We heard the headline band come on upstairs and headed up to check them out. Lucien led the way, Sharon, then me. Halfway up the steps, she reached back and took my hand. I was high from some strong grass, and the stairs were crowded, so I appreciated the gesture. In the main room, we wormed our way into the dense mass of bodies and were quickly wedged in tightly, Lucien still in front, Sharon, then me. I don't remember who initiated contact, but my hard-on was lodged tightly against her foam rubber ass. As the band played, her hands rested casually on Lucien's hips in front of her, and she gyrated to the rhythm, probably against him, definitely against me. I nearly passed out.

————————————

"Melodrama suits you well." I sang along off-tune as we drove along the Bosporus coast road late one night. I was at the wheel, Azine, our navigator, in the passenger seat, Lucien and Giles in the back. We'd just left a nightclub up in the hills north of the city and come back down to the shoreline to go back into town. We cruised around a curve and sighted a long line of taillights backed up in front of us.

"Hang on, what's this?" I asked jovially, taking a rough stab at an English wide boy accent. I braked and slowed down as we came up to the end of the queue. We all took a look to see what was going on. Azine quickly sussed it out, as apparently police checkpoints where they breathalyzed drivers were not uncommon. This was not good. Not only had I had a few glasses of champagne over the course of the evening and a toke, but much more significantly, I had a small bag of grass in my pocket. Not good at all.

My knee-jerk reaction was to make a U-turn and find another way back into town. But the police, as they do in the States, had chosen a spot where you couldn't see the checkpoint soon enough to do that inconspicuously. Reinforcing this were policemen wandering up and down the line of waiting cars eyeballing the occupants. There seemed to be a small army of them, and as in a number of countries, they came off more like soldiers than cops, with automatic rifles hanging from their shoulders. I saw that my best option was to stay as calm as possible and not do anything panicky. There was the question of whether to try to get rid of the marijuana. Attempting to surreptitiously drop it out a window seemed like a bad idea. Trying to slip it under a seat or somewhere else in the car seemed like it might attract attention. Leaving it where it was seemed like the best option. There was also the not insignificant issue of drunk driving.

I consulted Azine, trying to make it appear, for the benefit of our uniformed company as if we were just casually chatting. I didn't apprise her of my contraband problem. She asked how much I'd had to drink and indicated I might get the benefit of the doubt as a foreign tourist. She also said that when there were lots of cars, the police tended to be a little less strict. I sensed my passengers were all a bit concerned.

We were about three cars away when I saw how they were handling it. A cop stood in the middle of the road with a fistful of breathalyzers, giving one to each driver and making them blow, then glancing at it and either waving the car through or sending it to the shoulder where there were other officers. He had a bin at his feet where he threw away the used breathalyzers. I was nervous in the extreme, but knew I had to project being at ease as much as I could muster and plunge ahead.

Not to be melodramatic, but this cop was right out of *Midnight Express*—big, fat and ugly, just like the horrifying prison guard in the film. Because I'd brought grass into Turkey (not a risky direction for carrying drugs), Lucien had already made a few cracks to me about the film and the prison guard during our visit.

Our turn came and I pulled the car up. The cop eyed us with a scowl. I made sure he had a good look at my western face through the open window, and Azine leaned over and spoke Turkish to him, though there wasn't much to say. He held out a plastic whistle-looking thing and pulled back the cellophane wrapper as I took it. As nonchalantly as possible, I blew medium hard, not wanting to pull my wind to obviously. I handed it back to him. He glanced at it and paused for a couple of distinct moments. A major jolt of panic shot through me, and my body broke out with sticky sweat. The cop gave me a dirty look and waved us on.

Yes! Relief! I drove off as casually as I could manage, but as soon as we were out of sight, we whooped it up with shouts of "Davey the Bull" and "Kee-bob" coming from the back. I filled everyone in on my possession problem, making them all groan and shake their heads.

It was almost as if our visit to Istanbul was charmed and nothing could seriously go wrong.

Later that night, after a full hush had descended on

the city, Azine took us to an atmosphere-laden cemetery deep in the labyrinthine metropolis. I find cemeteries esthetically pleasing (like trees and elephants). This one was surrounded by a high stone wall and was unique in that the gravestones were upright obelisks contoured vaguely like coffins. The monuments were seven or eight feet tall, sculpted and ornamented in various intricate ways. They evoked people standing in repose, row upon uneven row of them, and cast long shadows in the moonlight. Spectral in their presence, stately and dignified. They exuded the passing of the ages.

———————————

October 1994.

One Saturday afternoon in New York, I was hanging out with Lucien at the bohemian-feeling sublet he'd recently moved into. The esthetic of the apartment was somehow suggestive of a macabre Egon Schiele painting. It was in an old shipping building near the Fulton Fish Market, pre-gentrification, on an uneven cobblestone backstreet with the Brooklyn Bridge looming overhead off to one side. I was sitting on the couch looking through a coffee table book of photographs of Charlotte Rampling while he did something around the apartment.

"Hey," he said, "I just got a letter from my friend Earl in England." He pointed to some typed pages on the low table of rough-hewn planks in front of me. "Give it a read. You might find it amusing."

The missive was more a creative writing riff than a letter. Toward the end of it, Earl wrote:

> *I was down at the Duke of Lonsdale having a few pints, chatting up this girl. And she says to me, "So, what do you do?"*
>
> *"I'm a hornithologist," I says.*
>
> *She looked a bit confused for a moment or two, but then brightened and said, "Oh, that's the study of birds, innit?"*
>
> *"Exactly, luvvy," I said, broadening my accent for effect.*

That's a tiny but not horrible example of one of the threads of life that Lucien and I thoroughly enjoyed, occasionally to the dismay of others. Thinking-man's vulgarity. The combination of the examined life—the struggle to understand and make sense of it all—with the rude and the crude. A lot of intelligent people revile vulgarity, see it as beneath them, having no place in their polite civilized existences. And I suppose most vulgarians don't spend a lot of time struggling to understand life or seeking out enriching experience. The divide is a shame, though, because the vulgar is a very real part of being human, inside most of us, whether we want to admit it or not. Often funny, frequently interesting, almost always connected to the core, the primal. It deserves the scrutiny of the intellect, is a worthy subject for humor, art and reflection. It has everything you could ask for—humanity, sex, feeling, complexity, and of course comedy.

Lucien and I fully appreciated both the thinking and vulgar parts of life, and were delighted when they blended.

There are a number of novels that are excellent examples of thinking-man's vulgarity. The leading writer in the genre has to be Martin Amis, who entitled one of his novels *Dead Babies*. Here's an example of his stirring prose:

> *It was when the patch of shit appeared on the pilot's cream rump that Richard knew for certain that all was not well. This patch started out as an islet, a Martha's Vineyard that soon became a Cuba, then a Madagascar, then a dreadful Australia of brown. But that was five minutes ago, and no one gave a shit about it now. Not a single passenger, true, had interpreted the state of the pilot's pants as a favorable sign, but that was five minutes ago, that was history, and no one gave a shit about it now, not even the pilot, who was hollering into the microphone, hollering into the world of neighing metal and squawking rivets, hollering into the very language of the storm its fricatives, its atrocious plosives. The gods had put aside their bullwhips*

and their elemental rodeo and were now at play with their bowling balls clattering down the gutters of space-time. Within were the mortals, starfished from white knuckle to white toe joint, stretched like Christs, like Joans in her fire.

Lucien turned me on to two other authors exceptionally accomplished in the genre—Will Self and Edward St. Aubyn. In the opening passage of Will Self's *My Idea of Fun*, the narrator describes his idea of fun—decapitating a homeless man and having sex with the neck of the headless body. The following is a blurb from *The Evening Standard* that appears on the jacket of the book: "Will Self's first full-length novel is the most loathsome novel I have ever read. I read it twice to make sure and am oppressed by a sickening, fatalistic feeling that I may soon read it again." Lucien gave me a copy of the book, inscribed, "To cerebral surfing on a sea of sycophancy."

There are also several Fellini films that capture circus-like swirling mixtures of the intellect and the grotesque, the sophisticated and the ribald.

The phenomenon makes plenty of appearances in everyday life. Different people pick up on different things, and Lucien and I moved through life noting the bawdy around us and in ourselves. We observed and made observations, took things in and gave our take on things. Our conversation was laced with wry vulgarity. *Drop 'em, blossom. Show us yer growler.* Remember? It was part of our sensibility, sprinkled throughout our patter, our banter. As Saul Bellow wrote, "Each man has his batch of poems."

Lucien went through one phase when he regularly called me "cunty." I might answer the phone and hear his deep mellifluous voice cheerily greet me, "Hello, cunty." In the States, of course, cunt is one of the few curse words that has retained its full force. Like when the Joe Mantegna character in *Glengarry Glen Ross* blasted the first-run theater audience back in their seats by screaming across the stage at another character, biting off the words, "You…stupid…fucking…cunt!" (Hey, as people say, Mamet has a real ear for dialogue.) But in England, the word has slipped into common usage and lost much of its ugly power. They say, "Don't be a cunt," the way Americans might say, "Don't be an asshole," or "Don't be a dick." I've even heard women in England regularly use the word. They don't seem to view it as the ultimate one-word put-down of females, as birds in the States do.

There was also the phase when he regularly addressed me as "You—ugly—bastard," drawing out the words with lip-curling emphasis. And sometimes when I'd come out with a bit of crudeness, he'd look at me and say with a sarcasm-dripping sneer, "You're a real charmer, Davey boy. A real charmer."

Then there was the period when he got in the habit of tightly squinching up his face and bleating in a high whiny voice, "Fuck off," with almost a twitch as he said it. Out of the blue. For no reason. I originally assumed he'd lifted it from *Life is Sweet*, a film in which a bulimic teenage girl throughout the movie expresses the same sentiment in precisely the same way. But when I mentioned it to him, it turned out he hadn't seen the film. We rented it, and the similarity was eerie. Seeing the disturbed girl deliver the signature-like squawk again and again, with authority, gave him renewed enthusiasm for the phrase-spasm, just as it was fading from his lexicon. And it had a second coming, much to Sharon's chagrin.

"Hot soapy tit-wank." Another favorite. I took a particular liking to this one. It *is* very descriptive. And colorful. Conjures up a lovely robust image, something most straight men have thought about at one time or another, if not experienced. An excellent ice-breaker, too, as in, "Allo, luv. 'Ow's about a hot, soapy tit-wank?" Always a good way to get off on the right foot with tasty crumpet. Right up there with, "Fancy a bonk?" There was an especially busty Mexican jewelry designer we used to run across in the downtown scene, who we took to referring to simply as HST. Not so she actually tumbled, of course. And the Frenchies taught me some Gallic slang for the act. Something like *braulette español* and *cravate de notaire*. You never know when stuff like that might come in handy.

Azine, as elegant as she was, was especially amused by one of Lucien's raunchy lines. She must've been familiar with it from when they were together back in New York. He'd be hanging out somewhere, and some woman would be coming on strong to him or one of his friends, or even to some stranger as he watched, and he'd exclaim with his bawdy rasp, "Oo, she wants to meet the beast." Azine could mimic this charmingly, with a Turkish-inflected version of his already cartoon-ish accent, her inescapable femininity coming through. "Oo, she wants to meet the beast." She made me laugh.

In Istanbul, there were big billboards all over the city advertising a type of ice-cream on a stick called Magnum. The image consisted of an enormous pair of moist bright red lips about to take a second bite out of chocolate-covered vanilla ice-cream on a stick, with the cream-colored inside showing from the bite already taken. It was blatantly prurient, had zero subtlety. And we of course found it funny. Giles commented to Azine how overt the whole thing was, and she said the television version was even worse. Apparently, though I found it surprising for a mostly Muslim country, the TV version had the same big red lips sensuously taking the bite, and a voice-over saying suggestively in Turkish, "If you want something big and delicious, try Magnum."

Naturally, we had to try some, and soon the floor of our rental car was littered with Magnum wrappers, which led to one of our most juvenile moments. One afternoon, Lucien, Giles and I were driving back from a visit to the Black Sea. (Azine was off doing something else.) Giles encouraged my aggressive driving with exclamations of "Davey the Bull" and "Go, Kee-bob, go." On a long stretch of straight highway, we noticed, in a new-model car to our right, four cute college-age girls who looked Turkish and upscale. They took note of us and started giggling and flirting with us as the two cars sped alongside. We flirted back, laughing. Then, Giles, in an inspired moment, picked up a discarded Magnum wrapper, held it up to the closed car window for the girls to see, mouthing the words, "If you want something big and delicious, try Magnum." After several confused moments in the other car, with Giles speculating about how to embellish his pitch, the girls sized us up for what we were and sped off.

It's curious. The pleasure of expressions. Phrases, slang, a good line. I mean, what is it that makes a particular grouping of words appealing? You hear a phrase like "he's just a fast-talking Johnny," and maybe it grabs you, maybe you like the sound of it, though you don't stop to think why. Maybe it stirs your imagination, resonates for you, speaks to you. And the next time you see a friend, you say for no particular reason, but with *feeling* as if you did have reason, "Hey, you're just a fast-talking Johnny."

The appeal I'm talking about is similar to that of poetry, but in relation to a much lower form of expression, a sort of illegitimate half-sibling of poetry. Word images/ideas/sounds strung together in an interesting way. It's the thing that makes a phrase in a song leap out and grab your ear though you weren't really listening to the lyrics and maybe don't even know what the song is about. It may turn out that the song-phrase doesn't remotely mean what it suggested to you. There are some lines in a Dylan song, and I've never had the slightest idea what they mean, but I love them. "My warehouse eyes, my Arabian drums, should I lay them by your gate, or, sad-eyed lady, should I wait?" I have no idea what that means, but it knocks me out, conjures up a intrigue for me.

The pleasure of expressions was of course another thing Lucien and I had in common. We were both people who could say of a word that it was a "good" word. Our taste in jargon ran along similar lines, reinforcing our general rapport. There was that feeling of: *someone gets me. Thank god! What a relief! What a pleasure!* It was a deep-seated pleasure to find someone on whom your batch of poems wasn't wasted. (Sharon certainly didn't get Lucien's.)

And of course for Lucien and I, the pleasure of expressions was closely intertwined with thinking-man's vulgarity. At least half the verbiage that grabbed us, if not more, had some churlish flavor.

Out at night in a bar or club, Lucien might look at me and say with a veiled, hooded look, "You are bequeathed in suede."

Or I might say, "You have an ephemeral whinging aspect," or in a flat lifeless tone, "Kill the cat. Kill the cat." And he might grin his trademark grin and say, "Hey, let's bang on another E."

Or he might show up one evening, all dandied up, and pronounce with a smirk, "I must say I look devilishly handsome this evening." Partly because that's what he thought, but also partly because he just wanted to say it.

Sometimes he'd rub his hands together slimily, projecting his creature-like persona in full force, and whisper sibilantly, "Yes, my precious. Yes-s-s. My precious-s-s."

June 1993. Majorca. Early evening.

Matthew emerged from the house onto the outdoor terrace and proclaimed, "The firth thing I want to thay ith…I have a *big* dick." With the intonations of a flamboyantly gay black male. This, it turned out, was a spoken-word phrase in some high-energy dance anthem that had recently been big in the clubs, laid over a rhythm track in the opening segment and woven throughout the rest of the song in bits and pieces. "The firth thing I want to thay…The firth thing I want to thay…"

Lucien deepened my appreciation for something I was already semi-aware of from my time living in London—a lower-class English accent is exceptionally effective for bringing vulgar expressions to life, giving them extra *oomph* and zest. It has something to do with the way the English lower classes embrace their loutishness as a badge of honor, and the accent is a key part of it, to the point of laying it on extra thick. They love their slang and colorful expressions, revel in a bit of crudity.

"Oo, she's a right old slapper." An Englishman might come out with that if, say, he was sitting in a pub and a tarty-looking woman walked by, one who was a bit too plump and past her prime for the too-short too-tight skirt she had stretched 'round her rump. A right old slapper. Skidding deeper into the gutter, there's, "Oo, I'd like to slip her a length" or "I'm gonna give her a good seeing to." Or deep in the muck of the sewer, "Up the old dirt box."

For all their famed poshness, the English have a true talent for vulgarity, and a thick low-life accent can enhance just about any tidbit of uncouthness.

■ ■ ■

"Old enough to bleed, old enough to butcher." Cockney growl, lewd grin. Embracing the Philistine within.

173

CHAPTER 11

Back in my mid-twenties, I attended Wharton and got an MBA. During the summer between the two years of the program, I stayed in Philadelphia and worked at a small investment firm, and took a summer course to lighten my load in the fall. The lease on my apartment had expired at the end of the regular school year, and I moved in with my girlfriend of the time. Her roommate was away for the summer and had sublet her room to a dental student.

Not your typical dental student. Scott was somewhat of an ex-juvenile delinquent, the kind of wild kid who in high school regularly got into trouble, pushed the limits. (Not unlike Roddie Baines.) It sounded vaguely as if he'd gone too far on a couple of occasions—joyriding/

car theft, possibly burglary—like maybe he would have been sent to a juvenile correctional facility if he'd been caught once more. But he'd been lucky.

He was a good-looking guy, very muscular—had a bench press in his room and regularly worked out with that and free weights. Took a lot of vitamins, including extra-large doses of niacin. He said he liked the way it made his body flush with heat.

He told me that when he was an undergrad, he and a friend would sometimes stage fake fights in restaurants, highly realistic ones with tables and chairs knocked over, meals flying to the floor. Their idea of fun. He wound up going to dental school because he was smart enough to get in and wanted to end up making decent money.

Not my kind of guy, but there was something appealing about him. He had a certain crude charisma. And he had an interesting, if weird, take on life, and wasn't without insight.

He was an extreme womanizer and regularly went out to bars by himself to pick up women. He preferred going solo. "If I go out with a buddy," he said, "I won't pay attention to the conversation. I'll be looking around the whole time. And I'll leave him alone for big chunks of time, off chasing skirt. Sometimes disappear completely."

As for the women, he had a good line of bullshit and could definitely be entertaining. He tended to go down the socio-economic ladder, maybe harking back to his eastern Long Island roots. "Malls are great pick-up places," he told me. He had a lot of one-night stands.

His bedroom was next to ours, and the walls were thin. We often heard rhythmic creaking and moaning. I heard him come in late one night with a woman, but there wasn't a lot of noise afterwards. The next day, when he and I were alone, he said, "Oh, man. She was a nurse. Good-looking. And she didn't play games. Didn't pretend like she didn't want to come back with me. She was all right. But when I got her clothes off, she had this bag and tube hook-up going on down below. She let me know it was okay to go ahead. But by then, I was pretty much turned off. Wasn't really interested anymore. But I could tell she'd feel really bad. She wanted to do it. So, I went ahead and screwed her."

I was surprised to hear that the woman's feelings had even been a consideration for him.

There was something slightly off about him. You just didn't know how far he'd go. For instance, it was clear some fairly kinky things were going on in his bedroom, and my girlfriend and I found ourselves wondering whether somewhere down the line something a bit too out there might wind up happening. Quests for kicks tend to go further, deeper.

Despite all that, I found him oddly likeable. One hot evening, we went swimming at the public pool in our neighborhood, which was surprisingly clean and not overly crowded. We sat on the side of the pool, our feet dangling in the water, and he told me about a time when he was a senior in high school, and he shared his girlfriend with a guy friend of his.

"She was one of the hottest girls in school," he said. "And she and my friend Brad always had this flirty thing going. They both owned up to being attracted to one another, like if she wasn't with me, they'd hook up. But I could tell they weren't going to do anything behind my back, so I was okay with it.

"Anyway, one day, I got it into my head that I wanted to experience her having sex with another guy. It wasn't specifically her. It would've been whoever my girlfriend was."

He didn't elaborate on his motives. It struck me that maybe he felt a compulsion to cauterize his emotions.

"She resisted when I first told her I wanted to do it," he went on. "But I pressed hard. You know, I'm pretty much about me all the time. Eventually, she agreed. Reluctantly, but she agreed. Getting Brad on board was no problem.

"I arranged for him to be at my house one afternoon, waiting in my bedroom. My parents weren't home. And my girlfriend and I drove up, parked in the driveway. She wouldn't get out of the car at first. It took about five minutes to convince her to go in. Then, we went inside and upstairs to my bedroom. And they fucked."

He stopped talking for several moments. I looked at

his face carefully for signs of feeling but didn't detect any. Maybe because it had occurred years before, maybe not.

"I watched my friend fuck my girlfriend. I watched them kiss. Tongues. Watched him suck her nipples. Watched her suck his cock. Watched him enter and fuck her.

"But the funny thing was, a few minutes into it, I went into the bathroom and threw up. I came back out and watched more. Didn't regret it afterward. But I did puke."

———————————————

I'm not sure exactly what made me think it in the first place, but sometime around the beginning of the summer of '94, it crossed my mind that maybe Lucien actually wanted me to. Lust after Sharon, that is. Be tantalized by her. Maybe even have sex with her. I mean, if something along these lines were true, how far did it go?

It didn't really fit my perception of him, but people are strange. We have hidden parts that sometimes we're not even fully aware of. "We are all queer fish," Fitzgerald wrote, "queerer behind our faces and voices than we want anyone to know or than we know ourselves." Maybe Lucien was just toying with the sensation. Or maybe it was just my overheated imagination at play, trying out wild thoughts, thinking *what if?*

I could never figure why he put up with Sharon's

outrageous behavior in the first place. He tolerated her flirting, her cock-teasing, much of it going on right in front of him He rarely showed the slightest reaction. Always stayed composed, casually hanging out, talking to people. He had the Brit sangfroid in him.

Sharon obviously wanted him to react, and to some extent his impassiveness may have simply been a refusal to give her that. But that didn't seem like the whole story. What else might be going on? Ego-tripping? Having everyone else get turned on by his woman? Or was it some kind of voyeurism? Maybe they had really hot sex afterward. She always circled back to him after she made her rounds.

None of this really rang true, though. But the thoughts did run through my head.

January 1994. NYC.

Lucien and I were out one night, and I asked him the classic question: What did he think the purpose of life was?

"The pursuit of sensation," he responded without hesitation.

This sounded very similar to the pursuit of experience, the answer I'd heard a number of people give over the years. But his choice of the word "sensation" seemed specific, and I wondered whether he was making a distinction between "sensation" and "experience".

Soon after, by coincidence, I re-read *The Picture of Dorian Gray* and saw that was very likely where he'd come up with his wording. The novel is, of course, the classic story of an extremely beautiful young man, Dorian Gray, whose portrait is painted and who off-handedly wishes, without remotely thinking it possible, that the portrait would grow old instead of him, that he'd always stay as young and handsome as he is in the painting. He even exclaims, in Faustian tradition, that he would give his soul for it. The book is about his wish coming true and how the blessing is in many ways a curse.

The other main character in the novel is Lord Henry Wotton, an extremely cynical jaded sophisticate, who spiritually seduces and corrupts Dorian, who plants in him the intense desire to stay young and gorgeous, esthetically pleasing to the world. Lord Henry believes devoutly in embracing all esthetic pleasures, seeking out new and delightful "sensations", in total self-indulgence.

The resemblance of the novel's ideas to Lucien's was much too specific, too strong, to be coincidence. And Lucien was very Lord Henry-like. When I next saw him, I told him I'd discovered one of his big influences, and he readily admitted it.

Lord Henry was a man who, in the words of the novel, "set himself to the serious study of the great aristocratic art of doing absolutely nothing."

Lord Henry's signature way of expressing himself was to toss off witty epigrams, many of which contained blatant paradoxes that revealed cynical truths. "The only difference between a caprice and a life-long passion is that the caprice lasts longer." "The only way to get rid of a temptation is to yield to it."

You could never be sure how much of Lord Henry said he meant. I suspect he would have said every word of it, or none of it at all, depending on his whim at the time. Sometimes he threw out one of his provocative remarks, and then "played with the idea, and grew willful; tossed it into the air and transformed it; let it escape and recaptured it; made it iridescent with fantasy, and winged it with paradox." After one particular remark, he "struck a light on a dainty silver case, and began to smoke a cigarette with a self-conscious and satisfied air, as if he had summed up the world in a phrase."

Lord Henry believed in making one's own life a work of art, that "now and then a complex personality... assumed the office of art; was indeed, in its way, a real work of art. Life having its elaborate masterpieces, just as poetry has, or sculpture, or painting."

The core of Lord Henry's beliefs was as follows:

Human life—that appeared to him the one thing worth investigating. Compared to it there was nothing else of any value. It was true that as one watched life in its curious crucible of pain and pleasure, one could not wear over one's face a mask of glass, nor keep the sulphurous fumes from troubling the brain, and making the imagination turbid with monstrous fantasies and mis-shapen dreams. There were poisons so subtle that to know their properties one had to sicken of them. There were maladies so strange that one had to pass through them if one sought to understand their nature. And yet, what a great reward one received! How wonderful the whole world became to one! To note the curious, hard logic of passion, and the emotional coloured life of the intellect—to observe where they met, and where they separated, at what point they were in unison, and at what point they were at discord—there was a delight in that! What matter what the cost was? One could never pay too high a price for any sensation.

Lord Henry urges Dorian, "Be always searching for new sensations." And Dorian, after he is fully corrupted and has practiced Lord Henry's beliefs for many years, with the benefit of his immutable beauty, finds himself engaged in a continual "search for sensations that would be at once new and delightful."

One afternoon at my loft, Lucien and I were talking about the book, and he skimmed through a copy of it as we spoke and pointed out a Lord Henry-ism he found particularly amusing: "Women, as some witty

Frenchman once put it, inspire us with the desire to do masterpieces, and always prevent us from carrying them out."

I suspect that before Lucien encountered the novel and its ideas, he was already on his way to forming insights and perceptions similar to those of Lord Henry's. So when he first read the book and encountered its concepts and beliefs, so similar to the ones emerging in him, articulated so candidly and clearly, it must have been quite a shock for him, inspiring and reinforcing. It brought his nascent life philosophy into sharp focus.

Ironically, within the story of *Dorian Gray*, there's another book that plays a key role in Dorian's life, the title of which is never given. Lord Henry gives a copy to Dorian, and it contributes to Dorian going down the path of decadence. "It was the strangest book that Dorian had ever read. It seemed to him that in exquisite raiment, and to the delicate sound of flutes, the sins of the world were passing in dumb show before him. Things of which he had dimly dreamed of were suddenly made real to him. Things of which he had never dreamed were gradually revealed.

For years, he could not free himself of the influence of this book. Or perhaps it would be more accurate to say that he never sought to free himself of it…The whole book seemed to him to contain the story of his life, written before he had lived it."

Lucien informed me that the un-named book was *Against Nature* by Joris-Karl Huysmans. There was still an English translation of it in print, from the original French, and he presented me with a copy as a gift, inscribing it. "To every emulation and a number of other pleasant sensations."

At first, I thought he was referring to himself and Lord Henry, but later it occurred to me that maybe he was alluding to another emulation.

———————————

From reading *Dorian Gray* and drawing on my own life experience, I realized that the sensations Lucien sought might not be all pleasurable. Which added to my thoughts about his complicity in my and Sharon's flirtation.

He certainly wanted new sensations, ones that took him out of the ordinary. It could be that he wanted certain disturbing sensations, as well. Pleasure-seeking often branches out into more decadent darker stimuli that push buttons deep inside, engaging you fully, maybe mixing blissful sensations with sickening ones. ("The palace of excess leads to the palace of access.")

I wondered whether Lucien, like Lord Henry, was investigating "life in its curious crucible of pain and pleasure," was seeking "a poison so subtle that to know its properties one had to sicken of it, a malady so strange

that one had to pass through it if one sought to understand its nature?" Was seeking the "great reward" of
sensation.

I also wondered, if Lucien aspired to Lord Henry-like
qualities, then where did I fit in? Me, with my endless
quest for lost youth.

My own variation on the pursuit of experience was the
pursuit of *being interested*.

As I was growing up, from a very young age I experienced regular bouts of intense boredom to the extent
I felt it was an illness, an oppressive soul-numbing condition. Malaise, ennui, dullness—a deadening, potently
unpleasant feeling. (I've read that Graham Greene, in his
adolescence and on and off thereafter, suffered in the
extreme from boredom and related depression, which
together he referred to as melancholia.)

I struggled over the years to escape boredom, which
literally speaking is achieved by attaining the state of
being interested. Flip sides of the same coin. So I actively
sought out the state of being interested. Figured out
what interested me and how best and most often to
experience those things. I concluded that the sensation
of being interested was one of life's fundamental pleasures, if not the most fundamental one. Being absorbed,
engaged, fully in the moment. Along the way, I tried
all the conventional ways of being engaged, being

entertained, and eventually some of the more decadent and detrimental "ways of escape" (as Graham Greene called them).

Along with this thinking came the realization that being an interesting person enhanced my ability to be interested. Being an interesting person increased my chances of having interesting experiences and my ability to appreciate them. And in turn, having interesting experiences enhanced my ability to be an interesting person. The two things fed off one another, creating an upward spiral growing ever taller as I kept feeding it.

As things turned out, though, and it's disappointing to admit, an overly simplistic early understanding of the challenges and complexities of life, combined with a fear of life consequences, ultimately held me back and channeled me into a fairly straight and narrow path. I ended up with a somewhat conventional life, successful by many people's standards, but boring to me. And so, when my life began at age twenty-nine, I resumed seeking ways to be interested, sometimes desperately.

July 1994.

It was approaching dinnertime in Wainscott one Saturday evening, the last weekend before Lucien left for his rambling travels that would ultimately lead to Istanbul. Sharon had been driving me crazy all day long. Not annoyed crazy. Horny crazy. That's what being around her was like for me. She'd been lounging around topless, playing with her nipples, tossing her hair, pouting her lips. Touching my arm when she spoke to me, making sure I caught glimpses of the little silver ball on her tongue. As familiar as it all was, it worked. That's the way guys are—easy.

Some of our group was focused on food preparation, others relaxed around the house. Music filled the common areas: The Waterboys, *That was the River, This is the Sea*. Some folks were drinking blended concoctions of strawberries, bananas, vodka and ice. Matthew sat on a stool at the island in the middle of the kitchen, in the midst of the cooking activity, painting a watercolor postcard, lost in his own world.

Sharon was taking a nap in her and Lucien's bedroom. Dinner would be ready in about twenty minutes, and it was time to rouse her. Lucien lay on a couch in the living room reading *A Flag For Sunrise*, and I called to him from the dining area where I was scattering utensils on the table. "Hey, I'm going to wake Sharon, okay?"

"Yeah, fine." He didn't look up.

I knocked and opened the door. She was asleep, sprawled on her stomach, half wrapped in a towel, sheets off to the side. I walked over and said quietly, "Sharon," touching her arm slightly. She stirred and opened her eyes without raising her head off the pillow, looked at me sleepily, then closed her eyes again.

I don't know what came over me. Or rather, I do but

I don't. I reached over and pulled the towel up so that one of her heavenly buttocks showed. I stood there and looked. She lay there with her eyes closed. I reached over and lightly cupped her butt cheek. She didn't react. I squeezed gently, massaged slightly. My entire person pounded, my mind swirled with arousal, implications, imaginings. Sensations coursed powerfully through me. Lucien was in the other room, my girlfriend in the kitchen. And this…this wonderfully toned, warm embodiment of desire lay there in front of me. I felt her raise her ass ever so slightly. I slipped my hand down between her thighs and felt her bushy moist opening. Pressed my finger there for a moment. It felt like all the blood vessels in my brain were going to burst. Then I said quietly, "Dinnertime," moved the towel back into place and left.

During dinner that night, Matthew said to me, "Understanding is overrated." I forget what I'd said to prompt it, though with Matthew the prompting might have come a day earlier, or a week. Or there might not have been one at all.

I gave him a *don't be ridiculous* look.

He looked back calmly and smiled, repeated, "Understanding is overrated."

This was sacrilege to me. Anathema. I'd devoted so much of my life to trying to figure things out. I'd placed so much faith in understanding, in the belief that it was essential to dealing with life, solving the problems that came up along the way, finding a satisfactory way of being. For me, it was never *ignorance is bliss*. I rejected Matthew's statement flat out: "You could not make a statement that was more wrong."

The debate continued on and off throughout the evening and into the next day.

In the beginning, Matthew wouldn't elaborate, stayed cryptic. "You may not see it yet," he said in a Confucius-like manner, "but understanding is overrated."

His refusal to present his case gradually had the effect of goading me to present it for him, which, after I got past the patent nonsense of his remark, I was vaguely able to do. "I get it," I said. "Sometimes it's better not to try so hard to understand, sometimes it's better to accept things and just live. Like Zorba. A lot of life is beyond our comprehension anyway. It's extraordinarily complex and random. We can never hope to have a true and complete understanding, so rather than beating our brains out trying to figure it all out in every situation, maybe it's better to sometimes just sit back and go along for the ride. Just have the experience, don't always try to understand, don't always need to understand. Accept and enjoy some things in life without fully grasping them. Accept some non-comprehension."

Toward the end of the weekend, I said to Matthew with a grin, "Hey, I think I'm beginning to understand."

Lucien weighed in at this point: "It's not understanding that's overrated. It's conclusions."

■　■　■

"Deeper. Deeper and deeper." The whisper, always the whisper.

CHAPTER 12

All in all, I never detected that Lucien had any significant psychological baggage. I mean, everyone has baggage, but he didn't seem to have any deep dark secrets. He was well balanced and generally content with himself, not inconsiderable things in this world. My girlfriend said of him once, "He's one of the most confident people I've ever met, but it's quiet. Not in your face. I guess that's what real confidence is like."

By the way, my girlfriend's name was Janey.

Snippets from his youth. From what little I know.

When he was a boy in Peru, living the life of a diplomat's child, his family had a housekeeper named Mercedes. When he misbehaved, and I'm sure he was a handful, her standard punishment was to make him sit for several minutes in the broom closet where it was pitch black when the door was shut. Her special touch, which in hindsight Lucien quite admired, was that when he was in the kitchen with her and she found a spider, she'd make a big show of putting the live spider in the broom closet. Once, she even feigned putting a large struggling crayfish in there. Lucien never actually encountered any creatures in the inky darkness, but he powerfully believed they were in there and spent much of his sightless incarceration squirming and straining to detect the slightest sensation of movement against his skin.

He ran away once, like a lot of young boys, myself included. He told me he had a vague memory of hiding in some bushes near his house and watching the Lima police arrive and be greeted by his visibly frantic parents.

After his family moved back to England, he was sent to boarding school a first and had a brief, seriously unhappy period before he adjusted. One evening, he called his mother at home, catching her in the middle of a dinner party, and despondently informed her he was going to kill himself and was just calling to say good-bye. She became hysterical and the dinner party was ruined.

Later when he was a day student at another English public school, he and Giles and a couple of friends formed a rock band. Lucien dyed his then long hair electric blue and Giles dyed his bright red. One afternoon, with their bold new hues, they walked into the courtyard of Lucien's family manor and encountered Lucien's well-bred traditional grandfather coming out of the house from a visit.

"Hello, Granddad." "Hello Mr. Frith." The lads greeted him politely.

His grandfather blanked them completely, walked right past them to his car, his oxfords crunching loudly on the gravel.

Snippets from the map of his spirit.

One night, Lucien and I went to a party he knew of in the East Village. It was already crowded when we arrived. One of the Frenchies was there, and the three of us stood and talked. After a while, Lucien said something about seeing some tasty crumpet and plunged into the melee with a backward grin. He was single at the time, autumn '94. The Frenchie and I leaned against a wall and watched him go, and I said with a shake of my head, "Women love him. If I had his appeal, I'd kill myself. With promiscuity, I mean."

The Frenchie, who was not without insight, responded, "No, it wouldn't work that way. Because part of his appeal is that he doesn't abuse his appeal."

I laughed, wincing slightly.

"And part of your appeal," he added, "is that you *do* abuse your appeal."

Another night on a Greenwich Village rooftop, late, after carousing, Matthew and I lounged in canvas deck chairs, talking. We faced a dark jagged skyline. He said, "No matter how close Lucien gets to anyone, there's always a part of him deep inside that says, 'This is mine, and nobody else is going to get it.'"

Lucien once said to me, "In the end, I don't trust anybody completely." Not a foolish viewpoint in this life.

A birthday dinner for him at a Thai restaurant on Spring Street. He and a bunch of friends at a long table. He dandified extra for the occasion—cream-colored suit, sky-blue shirt, patterned scarf. I don't know how he pulled that shit off. It would've been Lord Fauntleroy on almost anybody else. On him, though, it came off as casual and as if he had some inside knowledge about what was appropriate for every occasion. My gift was a mix tape I'd made for him, and as a card, I'd dashed off a small watercolor of his unique visage, working from a photo. I devoted all of about five minutes to it, and to call my drawing naïve would be to wrongly suggest that the rough results were an intentional style. I added to, or maybe rather tried to disguise, the crudeness of my effort by going for an exaggerated likeness. I thought I'd vaguely captured something of his personage in a distorted way.

He looked at the painting with my birthday wishes

written below, and a grin came over his face. He said, in his best Lord Henry, "In ancient times, when the Roman Emperors returned victorious from foreign wars and re-entered Rome, their subjects lined the streets and cheered wildly for them as they passed. The adulation was so great it was as if the crowd thought the emperors were gods. And so the emperors had servants who stood behind them in their chariots and whispered in their ears, 'You are mortal. You are mortal.' Just to make sure the emperors didn't forget they were *not* gods.

"In the future, whenever I have a moment where maybe my head is getting a bit too big, I'll be sure to take out this masterpiece to remind myself that I, too, am mortal."

One other fragment, just an image really, a scene. Driving with him in the English countryside, near his family home, fast but controlled, an idyllic winding country lane lined with tall hedges on both sides. A song called "Gorgeous George" blasted from the car stereo, about a dandy: *"One hundred at your beck and call. So why'd you pick on me?"*

I could easily imagine him up on stage playing Mephisto in some German avant-garde cabaret production, gazing out at the audience, face covered with white greasepaint, eyes outlined in kohl, lips red, dressed in black tails and maybe a top hat. He was a performer, almost always *on* in a way, but naturally, without effort. He had a bit of the devil in him, in a charming way, more mischievous than dangerous. He was a scamp. An imp.

"You like being a dilettante, don't you?" I asked Lucien once.

He thought for several moments and said, "Well, I sometimes find that gliding through…an enriched environment can have certain benefits." He took a drag on his cigarette, then added, "And sometimes one's presence by itself can exude a certain something to the world."

"I suppose there's something exciting about being with a dangerous woman," Lucien said to me one evening in a quiet bar over beverages. It had come up in a round-about way.

The conversation had started earlier with him saying, "I dislike friends being judgmental. I want to be able to be myself with my friends without worrying about being judged by them. People in New York are much less judgmental than in England. That's one of the things I like about being here. And really dislike about being there."

"Yeah, I get that," I said. "After all, nobody needs freedom from judgment more than me." I rubbed the two-day growth on my face. "I know what you mean, though. It's not only a drag to feel a negative judgment from a friend, but almost worse, the negative judgment inevitably limits the friendship in terms of what you'll reveal, what you'll be open about. And how much do you get out of a friendship when you can't openly be yourself?

"There is a point, though," I continued, "at which everybody will get moral on a friend. I mean, if a friend rapes a four-year-old, you're going to get moral on him pretty goddamn quick. And moving down the spectrum, if a friend robs a deli at gunpoint, do you get moral on them then? To the point of turning them in? There's some place on the spectrum where everybody will get judgmental on a friend."

"Yes," Lucien nodded, "but I'm talking about things within the realm of regular life. Like cheating on a girlfriend. Which is ethically wrong, but still you don't want your friend judging you for it. You want your friend to allow you some bad behavior and not think less of you. Accept that you're human."

I took a sip of my vodka tonic and said, in a slight *non sequitur*, "I've always thought that most healthy relationships require a fair degree of congruence in terms of ethical framework."

"Yes," he said ruefully, "I learned that from Sharon Burke."

"But what kind of ethical framework does she have?" I asked. "It's more of a lack of one."

"What I mean," he said, "is you're in a situation with someone, and they can either do the right thing or the wrong thing. And if they do the wrong thing, you expect them to at least grasp why it might bother you, at least see where you're coming from, even if they don't agree, even if they don't accept that they did anything wrong. Not Sharon."

"Why put yourself in a situation like that?"

And that was when he said it: "I suppose there's something exciting about being with a dangerous woman." And went on, "To put yourself in a situation with a person with a flawed moral scheme, that's, well… that's a lot of things."

"But getting messed over by somebody is no fun. Ego humiliation is no fun."

"When you're with somebody like that, you have to desensitize your ego, which is a good thing. The ego produces…psychological unpleasantness that's different than real emotional upset—like wounded pride. It wouldn't occur if there were no ego. If you quiet down your ego, you care less about how people respond to you, and people have that much less capacity to cause you distress."

I thought of Dorian Gray's pursuit of unpleasant sensations simply to know them. *Poisons so subtle, maladies so strange.*

I asked, "So, is being with a woman who has a lot of

potential to do you wrong about learning not to care?"

He laughed. "Maybe. It *is* good to desensitize the ego in any case, not let it be such a powerful force in your life, show yourself it's not that important."

"Morality is overrated," he said to me on another occasion. "It stems from fear of the id, the instinctual side of yourself. And sin—sin is a challenge, a risk, an act of courage and imagination. Sins arise from need and instinct."

I can't say it made complete sense to me. But the observation struck me as the type of provocative remark which is a deliberate overstatement but contains some quirky truth. Lucien enjoyed making remarks like that.

He told me once that a woman we were both friends with, a female Frenchie, had been badly mistreated by her Parisian boyfriend. Lucien seemed to be referring to physical mistreatment, but when I asked for specifics, he got vague. Eventually, I said impatiently, "Yeah, but what actually did he do?"

He continued his evasion, saying only, ""Christophe has a *black* heart."

I finally said something to Sharon. I forget when and where, but quietly off to the side. I said, "You know, it's a dangerous game we're playing."

She smiled ambiguously, not otherwise acknowledging what I'd said or what I was referring to. It was the one and only time either of us actually put it into words.

■ ■ ■

"I like a bit of a cavort," he growled with his lowbrow accent.

CHAPTER 13

June 1995.

I came across a used book at a flea market that I'd never heard of, though I was familiar with the author, of course. *The Naive and Sentimental Lover* by John Le Carré. It intrigued me because it didn't appear to be about espionage. I didn't know he'd ever written a non-spy novel.

I took a chance and bought it., and the novel turned out to be one of the most impressive character sketches and portrayals of a friendship I'd ever read. It's a story of a great friendship between two men, one of whom brought Lucien strongly to mind, and the other one, sadly, myself. It is a pure literary work, intellectually very ambitious. I learned later that it was critically trashed when it came out and sold poorly. However, as I read it, and later re-read it, I was repeatedly amazed by its bril-liance and pathos.

The two men are Aldo Cassidy and Shamus (surname never given). Aldo, often referred to simply as Cassidy, is a "prototype for the middle-class Englishman pri-vately educated between the wars." He owns and runs a successful business in London making accessories for prams—footbrakes, canopies, chassis. He is bourgeois, "one of a row," "of the herd." A member of a dining club called The Nondescripts. An extremely careful, just-so kind of man, who has long endeavored to cushion him-self from "the cruel scream of life." There is almost no sensation in his life, no "impact."

"Cassidy lives in a vacuum," observes Shamus' wife, Helen. *"Poor Cassidy … He suffers from thoroughly unre-alized potential."*

Despite all that and an easily punctured veneer of mild pompousness, Cassidy is not without redeeming qualities. The encroachments of affluence and conven-tion haven't "yet killed the magic of the spirit." He's been "corrupted by civilization," but in another sense, he's still quite "innocent." He still has in him stubborn remnants of fantasy, of dreaming. *"Cassidy really notices things,"* says Helen. *"He's got a real eye, if only he'd use it."*

Shamus says to Cassidy, *"You've definitely a spot of divinity in you, I could tell it a mile off."*

At the outset of the book, Cassidy is "in the twilight of his thirty-ninth spring." He's driving by himself in his

Bentley, which he's exceedingly proud of, through an idyllic part of the English countryside on his way to look at an old manor house for sale. (*"Jesus,"* says Shamus, after the two of them meet. *"There's a hearse for a Nondescript."* And a few minutes later, he says to Helen, *"Cassidy's got a Bentley, a dirty big long one with a silver tip."*) The owner of the manor house has recently died, and the house is supposedly unoccupied. Cassidy is going to look at it without the estate agent. As he arrives, driving along the long winding driveway, he has the momentary illusion that the thick foliage behind him has cut him off from the outside world.

After parking, he walks around the stately old mansion "taking the feel of the place," the "hulk of a dozen English generations." Just as he is grandly imagining living there, he notices, much to his surprise, "a faint but undeniable curl of wood smoke rising from the western chimney stack and a real light, very yellow, like an oil light, swinging gently in the portico."

"Hullo, lover," a pleasant voice says. *"Looking for someone, are we?"*

Cassidy and the unexpected occupant of the house proceed to have an odd introductory conversation, with Cassidy noting in the course of it that the stranger's "voice was remarkably compelling. Dramatic even, he would say. Tense. Balanced on a soft beguiling edge. Cassidy detected also…a certain regional deviation possibly in the Gaelic direction, a brogue rather than an accent."

From the stranger's "handsome face dark eyes shone with the greatest animation; a Gaelic smile, at once predatory and knowing, illuminated its features." He was wearing "a black coat of the type favoured by Indian gentlemen, midway between a dinner jacket and a military blazer, but cut with a decided oriental flair. His feet were bare and his lower body encased in what appeared to be a skirt," but turned out to be "a very old curtain embroidered with faded serpents and ripped at the edges as if by angry hands. He wore it off the hip, low at the front and higher at the back like a man about to bathe himself in the Ganges."

Cassidy assumes the man is related to the deceased owner and indicates as much, to which the man vaguely responds by alluding to an uncle he was close to, gored to death in "slow motion" by a "terribly old" bull. The stranger also says, *"There's this fellow in County Cork calling himself the one true living God, have you read about him? J. Flaherty of Hillside, Beohmin. All over the papers it was. I wrote to him see, challenging him to a duel. I thought that's who you might be."*

They go inside the house and continue talking after a fashion. The stranger's conversation keeps taking disconcerting turns, and he has "sudden changes of humour," making him "unnerving" company for Cassidy. As they're walking along a dark, musty corridor, Cassidy sees a beautiful naked woman enter through a side doorway and vanish into another.

The stranger is, of course, Shamus. The naked woman, Shamus's wife, Helen. And as Helen eventually tells Cassidy, they're squatters. *"Voluntary squatters. Shamus doesn't believe in property, says it's a refuge from reality, so we go from one empty house to another. He's not even Irish, he just has funny voices and a theory that God is living in County Cork disguised as a forty-three-year-old taxi driver. He's a writer, a marvelous wonderful writer. He's altering the course of world literature and I love him."* Shamus is at work on his second novel, the big one, some eighteen years after his successful first one, which was *"all about university, and being in our prime and how rotten it is to have to go into commerce…, and about this undergraduate and his love for this girl, which was all he ever dreamed of."* Helen.

Shamus has a "brilliant, infecting smile," and "could just put on accents like clothes, he had the gift." In his own way, he's "a terrific innocent…looking for love all the time." *(Shamus flung out his arms. "Give us a cuddle, lover. I'm starving.")* "Ever since I've known him," Helen says dreamily, "he's been a complete enchanter. When we were rich, it was the maid, the garage man, the milkman. And when we decided to be poor again it was…just anyone… he magicked them all. It's the loveliest thing about him."

Shamus disdains the masses, the "proles", the "Many-too-Many, the compromisers for whom freedom is a terror; these are the backcloth for the real drama of life." Shamus himself was one of "a Few," to which you could only elect yourself. "The concept was to elect yourself very early, and be precociously familiar with death… To live always testing the edges of your existence, the extreme outlines of your identity…; man is invisible until the cold waters of experience have shown him who he is."

Shortly after Cassidy returns to his normal life, he and his wife attend a dinner party with their usual circle of conventional people, and in the middle of it Cassidy imagines Shamus appearing out of thin air saying, *"Isn't it a bloody bore? Urban proles having a compromisers' orgy."* Shamus *"simply hates the middle classes. They compromise the whole way along the line. With life, with passion, with well…everything." "He hates convention, he hates the blind acceptance of restriction and the voluntary imprisonment of the soul."*

Shamus believes "any fool can give, it's what we take from life that matters." He's written his own epitaph: "Shamus who had a lot to take."

He needs "impact", sometimes to the point of crashing.

Shamus completely seduces Cassidy in terms of spirit and soul. *"I've never met anyone like either of you,"* Cassidy says to Helen.

Later, Shamus takes Cassidy's hand and says, *"You've never seen the bloody daylight, have you lover?"* Then he asks, *"Who are you?"* still holding Cassidy's hand and

watching his face with an expression of great puzzlement.
"What have you got?"

"I don't know," says Cassidy, putting on a shy expression. "I'm sort of waiting to find out, I suppose."

"It's the waiting that kills you, lover. You have to go and get it."

Back in his normal life, Cassidy's until-then subconscious dissatisfaction with his deadened existence quickly rises to the surface. At his business, a report is read to him regarding a pram shock absorber, stating that "it has shown up badly on the testing floor … The action of the spring, confined to an airtight case, has caused overheating and in one instance actual combustion. Subjected to a simulated velocity equivalent to five m.p.h.—that is the maximum allowable pedestrian rate—the spring was observed to burst through the housing." Prompting Cassidy to think, *'Whereupon … it was a free spring, burst from its unnatural housing. A bouncing, jolly, vibrant spring with a life to lead and a heart to give.'*

Cassidy decides he doesn't want death anymore. He wants life. He's "been near to things all his life, and this time, come what may, he is going to touch them."

Cassidy and Shamus go off to Paris together for four delirious rollicking days and nights of adventure and nourishment of Cassidy's parched and stunted soul. "Each day commanded for Cassidy…the same blind walk from the predictable to the unimagined; an inward walk to the closed-off places of the heart."

"Life," says Shamus, *"exists only in excess. Who wants enough, for Christ's sake? Who wants the twilight when he can have the fucking sun?"* In a restaurant, he pours a pitcher of water over Cassidy's head in a baptism of sorts, shouting, *"For Christ's sake, grow you little weed, grow!"* Later, in a wild, drunken moment, he sings out loud and demands that Cassidy sing along with him. Cassidy says he doesn't know the words but would sing if he did. *"Jesus, who wouldn't?"* says Shamus, putting *both hands over Cassidy's face, and lifting it to his own.* "It's *singing when you don't know the words that tears your guts out, lover."*

Cassidy and Shamus come to love one another as only great friends can. Shamus struggles mightily to get Cassidy to go all the way with the life-giving, spirit-freeing transformation he's begun while Cassidy continues to be afraid of giving up the safety and security of his conventionally successful life. Shamus, in essence, wants Cassidy to come out and play, whereas Cassidy is afraid of too much "impact." Shamus wants Cassidy to break free and experience the full sensation of living even if it means pain as well as joy.

Numerous tensions and conflicts emerge in their friendship involving the relationship between art and commerce, the possibility that the two of them are warring halves of the same person, and the fact that Shamus is wracked by a sense of failure as an artist because he's been unable to produce a second novel for eighteen years after his first. All this wreaks tremendous havoc on the characters and makes for numerous pathos-laden moments.

"Shamus speaks: Those who love the world take it; those who are afraid make rules."

Helen makes Cassidy promise to never hold Shamus back, but eventually Cassidy asks Shamus to go a little bit easier, to which Shamus responds, *"Never."*

Early one booze-laden morning just outside Paris, Shamus and Cassidy are playing by a river, and Shamus throws a small stone at Cassidy, hitting him on the side of the head. Shamus expresses anguished remorse for his misdeed but whispers to Cassidy, *"You've got to love me, lover. I need it, honest. That's nothing to what I'll do if you don't love me."*

In an angry moment, Shamus says to Cassidy, *"Being a prole, you are the commercial hinterland of my genius."* And later he proclaims, *"Why I love you: worshipping prole. What more can a man ask? The roar of the proles at the door, dizzy faces…cameras click…It's all anyone wants. Queen, me, Flaherty, all of us."*

Cassidy responds, *"Christ you idiot you only have to walk into a room, tell a story, give them your rat's eyes, and they know, we all know, that it's you, Shamus; your world. You're our chronicler, Shamus, our magus. You've got all we want, the truth, the dream, the guts. Okay, you're*

impossible. But you're the best! You make it real for us, we
know how good you are."

In another quieter moment:

"Shamus," said Cassidy, *"about my soul."*

"I thought you had it out," said Shamus.

*"No, truly. Listen lover. I really do think I'm redeemable,
don't you? Now, I mean. Since I met you. I don't think it's
a hopeless quest any more, looking for it, do you? I know
I'm reluctant. I've got a lot of bad habits but, well you have
shown me the way, haven't you?"* Receiving no encourage-
ment, he adds, *"There must be something there."*

Shamus makes hell; he doesn't raise it. In an elegant
restaurant, he drunkenly concludes a botched, celebratory dinner by doing a sword dance on someone else's
table. To convince him to come down, Cassidy says, *"Let
me have a go...I want to do a sword dance."* But when
Shamus gets off the table, Cassidy doesn't take his place
and instead helps the waiters lead the drunken Shamus
away. *Shamus whispers to him, "You lying bugger. You
never will do that dance."*

Later that same night, in a suite at the Savoy in "Lon-
dontown" where Cassidy and Shamus are sleeping:
*"Here, no longer in his dinner jacket, lying in his own hotel,
is a bourgeois who gave his life in search of a dream...To
my left lies an artist broken on the wheel of his genius; a
galaxy of a man, but not organized."*

Cassidy struggles with all his might to "put a value on
himself," to escape the "awful dark." And his magnificent

inspiration all along the way is "Shamus, the taker and challenger of life."

As Cassidy approaches the crossroads as to how far he will go in terms of living life to the full, Shamus pulls Cassidy close to him, and *"Cassidy smelt Paris again, and the drink, and the garbage on the street; smelt the wood smoke from the fireplace lingering in Shamus' dressing gown and the sweat that was on him all the time; and whatever detachment he felt was gone, because this was Shamus who had once been Cassidy's freedom; and had loved him; who needed him and had leant on him; rested on him in his hopeless search; played with him by the river."*

The night at 2019, when our Istanbul quartet stayed up all night and wound up at Sully's house in the Turkish countryside as the sun came up. After the caravan of cars arrived at the remote locale, everybody milled around slowly in the early morning light, dazed, waiting to see what the plan was. Lucien and I stood near one another, looking around at the moonscape, drug residue swirling in our systems, and for some reason we glanced at each other and grinned.

"The journey continues," he said quietly.

I nodded and after a few moments said in a whisper, "Promise me we'll never stop having adventures."

"Never fear," he said with his impish grin.

In the course of the evening when Aldo and Shamus first met, they and Helen go on an excursion in the surrounding towns and countryside, lasting until very late, and Cassidy winds up staying with his new friends in the old manor house. As the three them are falling asleep in a room with a glowing fireplace:

"Shamus," Cassidy began, as dreams and visions pressed upon him.

"What is it, lover?"

"Nothing," said Cassidy, for love has no language.

January 1995. New York City.

At a cocktail party, Matthew introduced me to his uncle, a successful magazine journalist and author of a book on expatriate artists who collected in Tunisia and Morocco in the 50s. Matthew had spoken of him often and fondly, and he was someone I wanted to make a good impression on. After we were introduced, we stood with a couple of other people and talked. In the course of the conversation, he made a remark about the human condition, and I interjected, "As my dying father said with his last breath, 'I don't understand any of it. I never did.'"

He looked at me closely and said, "That's a rather weighty statement, particularly given the circumstances. Must be quite a legacy for you."

I almost continued with my fabrication but thought better of it and said, "No, actually that's not true. I stole that line from the closing scene of *The Boys in the Band.*"

Matthew's uncle chuckled and said, "Well, it's a good line anyway. I may use it myself sometime."

On impulse, I went on. "Actually, a lot of the things I say are plagiarized. My conversation is laced with stolen lines and phrases. Or maybe I should say borrowed since stolen implies I've succeeded in making them my own."

"I think a lot of people do that," he said graciously. "More than most people would care to admit."

What I said was true, of course. I am an enormous plagiarizer. At least, I incorporate a lot of other people's verbiage into my repertoire. In a certain sense, this book resembles more a patchwork of lifted items than some-thing originating from me. Lines from books, movies, songs. From Bobby S. Three novels and a film discussed at length, extended passages quoted. The book is chock full of other people's creativity. I'm like the mythical magpie collecting shiny objects. At times, I've thought maybe it's excusable as being like sampling in rap and hip-hop. I've grabbed a refrain here and a guitar lead there and mixed it into my own recording of life. But then, I've always thought of sampling as cheating.

Co-opting expressions is an extension of taking pleasure in them. It stems from appreciation, and being an appreciator can be a kind of talent in its own right if it's done with discernment. Being a connoisseur, an aficionado, doesn't seem like such a bad thing. But maybe it can go too far. Maybe I should be weaving in more of my own fabric instead of stitching in so many patches from others. And of course I desperately want to be more than just an appreciator of fine verbiage, more than a collage-maker. I'd like at least once in my life to originate a sentence or two that someone reads, then goes back and reads again, and thinks, *Damn, that's good.*

One night, Lucien and I were at the Tenth Street Lounge, and we were talking about the personal collages some of us assemble. He brought up the distinction the ancient Greek philosophers made between a posteriori knowledge and a priori knowledge—knowledge you acquire from directly having experience, and knowledge you acquire secondhand from being told about it or observing it. He said one of the key questions for the philosophers was whether you could acquire true knowledge from secondhand experience. Could you really know what it was to fight in a war if you didn't actually do it? (Stephen Crane did a pretty good job of it.)

That particular question didn't interest me much. It was pretty clear to me that people acquire genuine knowledge from both direct and indirect experience, though the former tends to be deeper and maybe more reliably truth-revealing. What did interest me, though, was the way our personal fabrics tend to be made up of both kinds of knowledge, especially in these modern times when we're bombarded with so much media. Our personal tapestries these days are elaborate inter-weavings of first and secondhand experience. Viewed in that light, my plagiarism doesn't seem quite so bad. All my secondhand experiences were certainly part of the ride, part of the perceptions and understandings that emerged along the way. Part of the story.

I recently read of someone asserting the validity of "recombinant, or appropriation, art." The phrase struck me as euphemistic bullshit, and I thought I'd rather call my attempts *plagiarism art*, though that may well be a contradiction in terms.

Maybe I should be less hard on myself. Or more so. Difficult for me to know.

Stories from our real lives don't occur in orderly chronological patterns; they arise haphazardly from the randomness and chaos of life.

■ ■ ■

"But Azine, he's your brother!" I shouted from the living room through the open door of her bedroom.

CHAPTER 14

September 1994.

I'm not sure why Janey told me. She didn't for a long time. The reason she gave was she wanted to persuade me to be more understanding of Sharon. Some of it may have been the urge to gossip, the desire to have interesting, even juicy, things to say. Another factor may have been the notion that the obligation to keep confidences doesn't cover significant others, though I don't know that I qualified as significant to Janey. Overall, when it comes to two young women competitive in the feminine ways, who knows what motives come into play? It is worth noting that Lucien never told me.

Sharon was date-raped when she was fourteen.

From what my girlfriend gathered, Sharon discovered at an early age that she had a strong, ego-pleasing sense of her own feminine allure. She grew up hearing her parents tell people with a laugh how she'd been flirtatious from the day she was born. At around eight or nine, she began to get a fix on flirting, beyond the intuitive. She began to know her power.

At eight, she started to wear makeup and dress with the intent to be provocative, to titillate. Her mother apparently enabled her. Before long, Sharon succeeded in looking distinctly older than she was most of the time. At fourteen, she was passing for seventeen. Without in any way trying to suggest she was responsible for the vicious crime inflicted on her, my guess was that she was a Lolita type as a youngster, discovering her special effect earlier than most girls, and regularly gave her power free rein. She told Janey that by the time she was twelve, she was only interested in older guys and the more grown-up lives they led, especially the night-life. She skipped over hanging out at the mall and other common activities of kids her age. She wanted to get to the "good stuff".

She met a local twenty-year-old guy. "Cute and hip, at least for St. Louis." Looking back later, she saw he was the exciting bad boy type. He invited her to go out to a new nightclub she'd heard about but naturally hadn't been to. He said he'd be able to get her in despite her age, "no problem." He knew the guys who ran the place. It was 1987, and serving minors wasn't closely monitored in a lot of places then. She told Janey that, in the days leading up to their date, whenever she thought about walking into the "hot new club," she squeezed her legs together in anticipation. I was surprised she was conscious of this detail and remembered it, and even more surprised that she confessed it.

She didn't have any problem with lying to her parents about where she was going or with whom, but even so, her parents wouldn't have allowed her to stay out as late as she would need. Telling them she was sleeping at a friend's house wouldn't have worked because she needed to be able to get back in very late undetected, which likely couldn't be done at a friend's. So, on the agreed night, at around eleven she climbed out the ground floor window of her bedroom and met the guy waiting down the street in his jeep.

Entering the club that night, she felt a sharp tingling thrill and was "totally impressed." She knew she'd found her milieu right away. Checking out the women, she knew right away she was going be able to easily compete in this world, would thrive in fact.

The guy brought her one margarita after another, and she quickly got drunk. Eventually, he gave her some kind of pill. And after she was well fucked up, he took her to a friend's apartment and raped her. She resisted, and he got forceful.

When Janey told me, it sounded like a nightmare, and I felt genuinely bad for Sharon.

She tried to keep it from her parents for a few days,

but there was no hiding how badly shaken up she was. They looked into pursuing it legally but decided against it for the usual reasons—proof problems in a he said/she said situation, and the horrific ordeal for her as the accusing witness.

For a while after I heard about it, I softened toward Sharon and was more tolerant of her. But over time, my shock and sympathy wore off, and in various situations I began to react again to the young woman Sharon had become, rather than the girl who'd been savaged. To my discredit, there were limits as to how much I was willing to excuse because of the hideous experience in her past. I'd long known I should be more tolerant in general. But I was a late developer in so many ways.

May 1994.

New York magazine had an article, spun from the snobby but accurate observation that Manhattan had reached a point where tacky people ruled the clubs. The article described how, in bygone eras, the tone of the most stylish New York nightspots was set by the upper classes—The Stork Club, The Copacabana in its heyday, El Morocco. (The places that helped give rise to the term *café society*.) And after that, there was a long run when the most glamorous late night venues, Studio 54 and the like, were dominated by people whose daytime lives were just as "fabulous" as their late-night party lives—successful artists, fashion designers, super-models, socialites, etc. Now, the article pointed out, the regulars, the people who were always on the list, who set the tone, were hairdressers, wannabe's and fashion-ista-poseurs. They devoted almost all of their time and energy to making the scene and staying on top of where the right spot was on any given night, to continually coming up with the hippest, most outrageous fashion statements possible.

The article simplified things a bit. Nightclubs, even the best of them, have always had their tacky elements. But it was true that people who were previously on the periphery, the hangers-on, had made it to center stage by the mid-nineties, and for fleeting moments during the dusky hours, inside the caverns of New York night-life, they were stars. And that's what they wanted more than anything in the world.

The article profiled a prime example—a twen-ty-year-old blond girl from Staten Island, who was described as being a "true natural beauty" and "a ten in terms of erotic allure", but with no polish or sophistica-tion. (I pictured one of the early Guess Jeans girls like young Anna Nicole Smith.) This girl was out in Manhattan hotspots almost every night and usually stayed over at her girlfriend's apartment in one of the numerous char-acterless high-rises on First Avenue uptown. Technically, she resided with her parents on Staten Island, but she never told anybody that and was rarely there.

She and her girlfriend regularly played at being bi-sexual or lipstick lesbians in public, hanging all over each other, especially in the clubs. In their social swirl, that was considered ultra-chic. And they made sure there were always guys with money around to buy them drinks and supply drugs, sometimes limousines, occasionally a sexy new outfit. This girl in particular understood fundamentally that there was a deal to be made for her company, her decorative effect. She was quoted as saying, "Guys are easy to string along, to get what you want out of."

The two girls were convinced they were leading glamorous enviable lives. And this despite the fact that the featured girl didn't even have a job and wasn't going to school. She derived every ounce of her sense of self-worth from her status in the clubs, convinced it meant something significant. When asked about her future, she answered vaguely that she was going to be a star, though the journalist noted she didn't say it with much conviction. When pressed, she said, "maybe a soap opera actress or something like that."

———————————

Sharon definitely had the whole pseudo-lesbian thing down. When she was in a club, she'd often choose another trendy beautiful girl and start dancing with her. If the other girl was responsive, it often led to dirty dancing and an excellent floor show. She got the attention she craved, in spades. Sometimes, she and my girlfriend played at the game. It didn't seem like it was really sexual for them, more like they were just trying to be super hip according to the mores of their world.

Early August 1994.

One night after Lucien left for the summer, I went to Club USA with Janey and Sharon. It was big and horrible with a spiral slide winding down from the balcony to the main floor. Sexy, scantily clad girls came shooting down every so often, to the appreciative roar from the crowd. Janey whispered to me that Sharon had worked there as a dancer on one of the raised platforms. I could easily imagine it—Sharon soaking up lust, driving more than a few in the crowd crazy.

The three of us walked up to the entrance to the VIP area, with Sharon in the lead. The guy on the door wouldn't let us in. Sharon immediately turned it on for him, cajoling, insisting and sweet-talking all at once. But for one reason or another, the guy wasn't having it. She wouldn't quit, though. Her approach usually worked well on the rare occasions when she needed it. She moved up close to the guy and put her hand on his chest. At this point, I said to Janey, "Come on, let's go. If the guy won't let us in, he won't let us in."

Janey suggested we give it another minute, and after a few moments, she leaned forward and put her hand on the guy's chest, began flirting with him.

I felt a surge of anger. I put my hand on her shoulder and said, "Come on, let's go." She may have been embarrassed at what she was doing, I'm not sure, but in any event, she conveyed to Sharon that it was time to quit, and we left.

Later that night, I said to her, "You put your hand on a guy's chest and flirt with him to get into a room? A *room*? Who cares? Who gives a shit? I don't care how Sharon behaves, but when you're with me, please don't demean yourself and me like that."

Lucien used to joke he was going to write a book called *Dirty Old Men* and devote at least a chapter to me. Sometimes I'd respond with a deep stagey growl, "What is it about a schoolgirl?" or "Thank goodness for little girls."

People focus a lot on the physical side of aging, but people age psychologically as well. As you get older, your personality slowly fossilizes. You become set in your ways; your quirks and idiosyncrasies become more pronounced. Your personality loses its fluidness. I've done my utmost to stay fluid. It hasn't been easy, but the results have made the effort worth it.

I was at the Edinburgh Theater Festival one August watching a play, and one of the actors on stage said in a thick Scottish brogue, referring to aging rock stars, "One day you have it, and the next day it's gone. You just lose it and can't get it back." I'm aware that may well happen to me, too, but I'm fighting like hell to stave it off as long as I can.

A lot of people stop hanging out when they get older. Not a lot older, either, just, say, more than thirty-five or so. I understand that hanging out in the nightlife doesn't continue to be as consistently fun as when you were young. I understand that people outgrow club life; it ceases to suit them, they're no longer prepared to spend large chunks of time that way. But a lot of people stop hanging out altogether, stop even minor outings like meeting a friend at a bar to have a beer, not to mention something more ambitious like going to a concert or something like that. A lot of people, guys in particular, basically stop having active friendships.

I hope like hell I never stop hanging out. When I'm seventy-five, I want to be the old guy sitting at an outdoor café in the Mediterranean, with brush cut white hair, wearing old jeans and a raggedy T-shirt (saying "She won't live" on the front, and "But then again who does" on the back), playing backgammon with a friend.

I'm sure that some people think my view that hanging out is an important part of life is downright silly, shallow and immature. But I see it as a key part of leading a vital life, and don't expect to ever change my mind.

Late one night, over a bevvie, I said to Matthew, tired but with feeling, "You know, that *Withnail and I* thing, I want to always keep some of that in my life. That last gasp of glorious havoc-wreaking irresponsibility."

In the end, I want to be able to say of myself, *he got down in the mulch.*

Azine said one evening to amuse me, "I worry about the worms."
Indeed.

■ ■ ■

"Beware of the Wasp Factory."

CHAPTER 15

"**S**top turning over your coffee cup like a wanker." Giles chastised me for acting like a tourist. He, Lucien and I sat at the Bebek café in the late afternoon Istanbul light, bright but soft on the eye. It was our last day. Lucien and I played backgammon—clicking and rattling, an occasional clack. It was peaceful.

"I've decided that the word to describe Giles is feral," I said.

Giles curled his lips back and showed his incisors.

Eventually, we took a last look around the simple but ideal café. Then strolled back to our nearby way stations to get ready for our last night.

For dinner, Azine chose a restaurant high on one of the hillsides with an open-air terrace. Our table was at the curved edge overlooking the Strait below.

The Bosporus—it was always there soaking into you, an enormous serpent of water. I felt envious of people who'd grown up with it being part of their everyday lives. I imagined an Istanbul native returning to the city after years of being away and first seeing the living waterway again—an intricate flood of feelings, an incredible sense of comfort.

Ultimately, the thing about Istanbul is the aura, the emanations. The place has an exceptional ancient-cross-roads-of-the-world vibe all its own, and you'd have to be completely insensate not to feel it.

The warm beautiful night enveloped us; there was a lovely breeze at our elevation. We ordered a bottle of Moet and I gave a toast. "To Azine. For allowing me to fall a little bit in love with her. And to Lucien, for making it possible."

After our feast, we collected ourselves and were off to visit the *gypsies*.

Mid-August 1994.

My last weekend in Wainscott before I went off to join Lucien in Istanbul was coming up. He'd been gone a little over three weeks. As I did whenever work allowed, I was going to drive out on Thursday evening and make a three-day weekend of it. Janey couldn't take Friday off from her salesgirl job, but Sharon was free—out of school for the summer, no regular job. She met me at the Avis office on East 43rd.

The night before, Janey had said to me, "Damn it. Why do I have to have a best friend where I have to worry she's gonna give my boyfriend a blowjob in the car on the way to the Hamptons?"

Much as I may have wanted it to be a possibility, I was pretty sure it wasn't in the cards. I was surprised Janey was concerned.

———————————————

The gypsy neighborhood in Istanbul is not some colorful tourist attraction. By no means. It's in the midst of a harsh rundown out-of-the-way part of the sprawling city. A truly alien world, well outside the scope of pleasantly interesting places that travelers usually seek out. Dangerous for outsiders, especially at night. But Azine had decided, as a treat for our last evening, to take us to a woman she knew there who would arrange for private belly dancing, the genuine article.

At the restaurant beforehand, Lucien and Giles started joking how risqué the show might get, and Azine indicated it would only be dancing. She also said we should behave ourselves. Gypsy men would be around, possibly brothers and husbands. Which made us start joking about knives. Gypsy knives.

———————————————

Sharon and I drove out the L.I.E., with me vividly imagining the act that troubled Janey. I tried willing it to happen.

It wasn't easy for Sharon and me to have a sustained conversation. The chances of me and Sharon having any form of actual sex seemed very slim, but I thought I should at least try to maximize them. So I worked hard to conjure up a facsimile of rapport, much like I did on dates where my only objective was seduction. My efforts fell flat, though. I couldn't get a feeling of connection going.

For her part, she made one of her occasional efforts to impress me conversationally. She knew that Lucien, Janey and others found me smart and interesting. A part of her wanted to be around smart interesting people; it just wasn't that big a part.

It was a blowjob-less ride.

Azine had trouble at first finding the turn to get to the gypsy district. We were already in an extremely desolate part of the city, and it was late. I couldn't imagine what it was going to be like at our destination.

"We're gonna get killed," I said jokingly.

Eventually, Azine recognized an abandoned overpass and directed us under it onto a dark street running alongside the base. The area could have been one of those gritty urban wastelands you see in New York-based crime movies, except the buildings were prefabricated-looking and the vicinity was even more of a shambles. I was high and drunk and beginning to wonder whether maybe we were doing something stupid.

Out of nowhere a neighborhood appeared—ramshackle wooden row houses, people outside in the dark narrow streets. Lights glowed from open doorways and small windows. The doors opened directly onto the street, no sidewalks. Men sat around in front of them on chairs and upended crates, most of them smoking, staring at us as we drove by, our windows down. There were other people standing in shadows off to the side.

It was past midnight, but there were plenty of people outside. The faces had a distinct look, seemingly a blend of Turkish/Middle Eastern with Slavic/Southern Russian, and a tinge of Mongol. Most of them had skin the color of tobacco, dark hair, gone gray or white on some, eyes slightly slanted. There were some extremely leathery faces. It struck me that this was indeed a neighborhood where people carried knives.

Kids were running around—genuine street urchins, I supposed. Some of the women could best be described as painted women—frilly turquoise skirt on one, bright crimson scarf on another, shiny gold bangles encircling their wrists, wonderfully garish makeup, a couple of them with incongruous bleached-blond hair. If they hadn't been right there and so real, they would have seemed right out of Central Casting. Two of them caught sight of Giles' curly blond locks and exclaimed out loud, pointing at him and touching their own hair. They beckoned to him.

We drove slowly through the maze-like streets trying to find the right house. People made vague offers to us, but Azine said we should stick to the plan. She also said that when we found the woman's house, we should park right in front; otherwise, the car wouldn't be safe.

"I'm gonna get killed," I moaned, continuing my attempt at humor. "I know it. I'm gonna get killed."

In my endlessly plagiaristic, observing-my-own-life kind of way, I had visions of the scene in *Sheltering Sky* where Port Moresby goes out walking at night in Tangiers and is lured down a dark hillside into a tent/shantytown to be with a prostitute, where he is attacked and barely escapes.

We finally found the house, and the woman came bustling out, enormously fat. As we got out, I said monotonously, "I'm gonna get killed."

"Oh, shut up," Lucien said with a grin. He turned to Giles, the crooked smile still on his face, and said with a stagey growl, "It's a night for vampires."

The woman arranged for one of the street kids to watch our car and hustled us inside.

———————————

Sharon was losing Lucien and knew it. As I mentioned, he'd been pulling away from her in his oblique English way, and his extended jaunt overseas without any discussion of her joining him was a big step in that direction. She tried to be cool about it, going on to Janey about misgivings and reservations she had regarding him—his lack of ambition and focus according to how she saw things, his lack of desire to make serious money. She tried to make out like it was mutual—the drifting away—but there were cracks in her façade. She didn't dissemble well. She loved him. Yes, for all her bullshit, she loved him. And rightly so. As I said to Janey on more than one occasion, he was the best guy Sharon was ever going to get. He was a fluke for her. I half-joked to people that Sharon was going to wind up living in a gaudy Beverly Hills mansion with some rich fat cat, leading the Joan Collins lifestyle.

During Lucien's absence, though, she was hurting. I actually felt a bit bad for her. Pain is no fun. And to see she had some real feelings, underneath all her crap, made me dislike her a bit less.

My dislike for Sharon was too much, probably more than she deserved.

As we walked from the car into the gypsy woman's house, a crazy thought formed in my inebriated brain— our running joke was true, and Lucien had brought me to Istanbul to kill me. Not so I believed it. More of a *wouldn't-it-be-crazy* kind of thought. But it did make me think that maybe somehow he *knew*, as unlikely as it was.

It *was* a neighborhood of knives. I could feel it. An image flashed through my head of a scimitar-shaped blade with an ivory handle, bejeweled and ornately carved.

I was clearly absurdly in love with the romantic notion that my life might somehow rise to experiences worthy of an adventure novel. I'd always wanted my life to have intrigue and be well outside the range of the ordinary. To include experiences that made me feel alive.

On the other hand, maybe Lucien did know something. There were telephones. And maybe inside he was harboring ferocious ill will toward me. I was extremely high, even for me.

───────────────

The titillating nervous tension of the car ride with Sharon dissipated as soon as we reached the house. Other guests were already there, old friends of mine from England, a couple with a beautiful mulatto son, Jasper, three years old. They had arrived earlier in the week when the house was otherwise empty and were staying through the weekend. It warmed my heart to see them. They hadn't completely recovered from jetlag, so we had a quiet dinner, played chill-out music, and didn't even drink a whole bottle of wine between us. The guy in the couple, a mischief-maker from way back, had met

Sharon before and had her number. He subtly poked fun at her all evening. But he wasn't immune to her charms, and it sometimes seemed as if his mild digs were a way to shut down other urges. After dinner, the four of us sat around the table talking for a little while. Then we all retired early. There would be more raucous evenings after the rest of the gang arrived the next day.

I'd told my English friends when they'd arrived to take the larger of the two downstairs bedrooms; they brought a portable crib for their toddler. I put Sharon in the upstairs loft, open to the living room below over a low wall, since she was solo and wouldn't need a closed-off room, while others would. The loft area was next to the master bedroom where I slept (with Janey when she was in residence). I told Sharon to use the bathroom just inside my bedroom door rather than going downstairs and up all weekend.

I used the bathroom first. Then with the bedroom door open, I lay down on my bed in only boxer shorts and tried to re-read *Brideshead* without much success. Out of the corner of my eye, I saw her slip into the bathroom. It looked like she was wearing a silky black camisole and matching shorts. She had to be aware of me laying there, had to be conscious of the situation. I was certainly acutely aware of her. When she came out, we said our good nights and she went out to the loft. She didn't close the adjoining door.

I lay there feeling the seemingly super-charged air

in the twenty-five or so feet between us. It might have been all in my head, but even if it was, the feeling was very real. What did she want? What…did…she…want? I suspected she wanted me to try. She wasn't going to encourage me or anything like that, much less give me a green light, but she wanted me to try. Whether or not she'd be receptive was another story.

———————————

In the gypsy woman's house, we were led through corridors to a long narrow low-ceilinged room. I don't recall any windows. At the far end was a wooden table and chairs. A bare light bulb hung from the ceiling. The woman sent a child to summon people from other parts of the house, maybe neighboring houses as well. I had the vague sense that the dwellings on either side were connected by interior doors. Excitement was in the air, not just for us but the gypsies as well. They had guests, foreign guests, and they were going to perform.

We were directed to sit in chairs on the far side of the table. Azine worked out the price with the woman, a ridiculous amount of lira. Lucien, Giles and I sat facing the room, the table in front of us, me in the middle. Azine sat unobtrusively off to the side. We were served beer and encouraged to buy some for the musicians, which we did. They trailed in, carrying instruments and chairs for themselves. Violin, clarinet, and standing drum. (Maybe an Arabian drum, who knows?) I wondered what relationship the musicians might be to the dancers yet to appear.

The flurry of activity died down. The musicians, sitting at the other end of the room, began to play. The clarinet in the lead unfolded a sinewy haunting melody, the drum provided a soft syncopated rhythm, the violin supplied texture and mood. They were good. The gypsy woman stood off to one side, looking quite pleased.

A plump young woman came in—large breasts, long dark hair, about twenty-five years old but with the bloom of youth already fading. A large, emerald-green scarf speckled with gold thread was tied around her hips as a skirt, showing some leg. Her feet were bare. Another multicolored scarf was draped around the back of her neck, crisscrossed her breasts, and was tied behind her back. Her midriff, of course, was bare.

She proceeded to belly dance. Undulating her stomach, swiveling her hips. Winking her navel, celebrating her flesh. Shimmying from head to toe. It was entertaining, but there was a certain going-through-the-motions air to it.

After her exit, a girl came in who couldn't have been more than sixteen. She was quite pretty with medium-length, dark-brown hair, dressed like the first woman in scarves and bare feet, but very innocent looking. She seemed slightly shy and nervous but relaxed as she started dancing. The drummer began to sing in a plaintive voice.

Part of me felt I should be horrified at the girl's age, but she was clearly proud of her moment. I speculated that she was at a stage where she was joining the family business, or one of them, a phase when she was becoming a woman according to her world. I imagined her as a child watching from the doorway, as other children were at the moment, and yearning for the day when it would be her turn to dance.

She seemed to enjoy herself, exuding a proud awareness of her budding sexuality and its charm. She was coyly flirtatious and began to experiment with more sensual movements. I was fully absorbed, if for no other reason than the strangeness of it all—this beautiful woman/child dancing sinuously in front of us, glowing softly in the night, in this alien city and even more alien enclave. The entire situation was so far removed from anything I knew.

The third young woman was the last. Midway between the other two in age, with a curvy youthful caramel-colored body. Exotic face. The most confident of the three. Dressed like the others but with her lower scarf folded up short, barely covering her hips.

She was a true performer. The music wove its spell. The gypsy woman clapped to the rhythm, which sped up. The young woman was wonderfully alluring. You could tell she moved by some completely attuned instinct. She swayed and whirled with a marvelous blend of feel and skill. She had a sensual earthy quality that seemed elemental, as if from another time. My head swam. My whole person swam.

She surprised us by removing her top, revealing plump firm breasts with peach-colored nipples. I noticed Azine look surprised. The girl gradually danced around the table to where we were sitting. She turned tail to Giles on my left, kept moving to the rhythm and gradually lowered herself onto his lap, the tempo picking up. She began to rotate against him, but he was unresponsive, and she reacted dismissively.

She sidled over to me and began to sinuously gyrate her beautiful rear end in front of me. I had a rock-hard erection. She lowered herself and pressed me into her delightful crevice and squeezed. I thought I might pass out. I was dimly aware of Azine and my friends watching me from close quarters. And the gypsies in the room, the men. Excruciatingly aware of the girl's firm buttocks clenching me, moving in circles. My arms hung loosely at my sides as I resisted the powerful urge to reach around and squeeze her breasts, pull her back against me. My head rolled back as I strained intently not to come.

Bizarrely, out of nowhere, I had a flash of coming, and at the moment of orgasm, the dancer suddenly disappeared and a shiny blade with an ornate handle passed in front of my neck from my right where Lucien was sitting. And was abruptly pulled back, slicing through the soft flesh of my throat. Blood spurted outward, my body started to twitch and spasm.

And then I came for real, the hallucination exploding into nothingness. The dancer re-appeared.

I got up from my bed and walked the distance between us, protruding in my boxers. The lights were out in the loft; behind me, the reading light in my bedroom was on. Sharon lay on her stomach, head on her pillow facing away from me. A sheet covered up to her midriff. I was sure she was awake, but she didn't react to my entrance. I sat down next to her on the edge of the bed. Still no reaction. I put my hands on the sides of her neck and began to massage. No response. Began to move my hands around. Kneaded her shoulders, back, sides, coming close to her breasts. Gradually, I went lower and lower on her back until the bottoms of my palms were brushing the tops of her buttocks.

I cautiously slid my hands down over her firm mounds and squeezed. She stayed motionless. I returned my hands to her back and, without interrupting the massage, moved so I was on my knees straddling her, raised slightly off her. I reduced my touch to a caress. Gradually sat lower and leaned forward. My cock pressed firmly against her. I kept thinking she was going to stop me, but she didn't.

I started to move my hips ever so slightly against her. Every nerve in my body was throbbing, and I stopped moving for several pulsing moments. Then I rolled off to one side, gently turned her over, and kissed her. She kissed back, not passionately but lukewarm, sort of go-ahead-if you-will. I wondered if I should stop. Her puffy lips were pliant in a wonderful way. I cautiously probed with the tip of my tongue, and her mouth opened. I felt her breasts. They were everything I'd imagined. Ran my fingers over her hard little nipples.

I rolled on top of her and pushed her legs apart, my mouth still on hers. Lodged myself against her, my shorts and hers still on. I thrust against her warm groin. My tongue went deeper in her mouth, and I felt her little silver ball. Sparks sprayed through my brain. Since my first glimpse of the tiny metal ball, I'd been dying to feel it with my tongue.

I shifted and slipped my hand inside her shorts. Her pelt, which I'd seen when she sunbathed nude in Majorca, was soft and downy. She was moist. I lowered my mouth to one of her nipples and pushed her shorts down. She was still reacting only minimally, but it seemed clear she wasn't going to stop me.

I probed with my fingers. Pushed my boxers down and pressed myself against her thigh. Stayed like that for a minute or so. Then slid on top of her and entered her in one continuous motion.

In the end, she did respond. Not wildly at first, but she began to move with my rhythm. Then began guiding my movement slightly with her hips. As I tensed and swelled, she began to buck. Hard, violently. Smashing herself against me. Seemingly in anger, not pleasure. I was surprised at her strength. As I came, she smashed me up off the bed several times.

I could tell it was over immediately. Something in her shut down. She hadn't come, I was sure. Janey had told me she had problems in that area. And I hadn't given her much attention.

I rolled off to one side. I had the distinct feeling she hadn't really wanted to do it but had let me anyway. Maybe to strike back at Lucien. Or maybe because empty sex was something she inflicted on herself every so often.

I lay there, feeling curiously guiltless. Maybe it was a feeling of, *Well, it happened and there's no taking it back.* Besides, at that moment, no one else in the world knew. It was as if it had happened in a vacuum, and outside it hadn't.

I'd done it. And had known I would if I could. The only thing that would've stopped me was her. I had to do it, or so I thought. It was who I was. In my silly way of always seeing my life in terms of books and movies, I thought of Valmont proclaiming again and again, in the course of his seductions, "It's beyond my control. It's beyond my control."

What about friendship? My great friendship with Lucien? Maybe if she'd been less overt in her provocations. Maybe if their relationship had seemed more like a real attachment, hadn't been on the verge of being over.

And poor Janey, nameless for so much of this book. With a boyfriend like me and a best friend like Sharon, she might as well drop a bomb on her life and start over.

I kissed Sharon lightly on the cheek, probably the only moment of tenderness ever to pass between us, and went back to my room.

CHAPTER 16

*L*a *Dolce Vita*. If I recall correctly, the film closes with a quiet but powerful morning-after scene that is quite moving. The story takes place mostly in Rome and is about an Italian journalist who gets caught up in *the sweet life*—the glamorous decadent lifestyle of the ultra-chic rich who project sophistication often with nothing behind the projection. The journalist is strongly drawn to the sweet life and yet vaguely repelled by it as well. On the last night in the story, he winds up at an impromptu after-hours party at somebody's beachfront house outside Rome. He stays up all night, and after everyone else has finally crashed in the blackout-curtained house, wanders outside to discover it's morning, a bright sunny morning.

He walks along the beach in the almost blinding

sunlight, carrying his loafers, his pants sloppily rolled up. I'm not sure what it is—the acting, the directorial touches, or the overall pathos of the film coming together. No words are spoken. But somehow, as he strolls along the beach, you sense him feel the complete emptiness of it all—the sweet life. Despite all its allure and glamour, *la dolce vita* wasn't worth a damn, wasn't worth more than a small portion of the valuable time which is your life.

It's strange, the feeling you get when you stay up all night and find yourself in the early morning light. A strange but interesting state of mind. Weirdly appealing. Wasted but with heightened lucidity. As if your blinders have been removed, all your walls are down, your receptors wide open. You can see life with a preternatural clarity, things you wouldn't otherwise see, maybe even some things you don't want to see.

I said my good-byes in Istanbul at three in the morning on the dark quiet main street of Bebek, in front of my hotel. I'd be leaving for the airport in a few hours. Lucien and Giles would be flying to England later in the day, where Lucien was going to stop over for a few days before returning to New York.

In my hotel room after the farewells, the last kebab

I'd sampled violently disagreed with me, and I hugged the toilet bowl for what little was left of the night. At dawn, I pulled myself together and drove to the airport, still feeling quite rocky.

I had had an incredible time, a jam-packed bacchanalian phantasmagoric ride, one of the best times of my life. It was reverberating in me and I knew it would continue to for weeks to come. But I had an empty feeling as well. Due in part to the return to regular life, the inevitable comedown. Also, heading to a big hectic airport for a long flight home in coach—not exactly an uplifting prospect. And floating through me like a fog was the knowledge that life can't always be an endless series of adventures. You can't always have the feeling of living life to the full. And maybe some of my deflated feeling was due to feeling endlessly caught up in the pursuit of the sensation of being alive. As long as I was in pursuit, there would always be a part of me that wasn't all the way there. The pursuit might have become such an integral part of me that I couldn't ever turn it off and be completely where I was, even if I'd reached the place I sought. Like doing cocaine, when you're always chasing the high; even if for brief periods you feel fully charged, you're acutely aware that the high will pass all too quickly and you'll soon be chasing again.

Most importantly, though, my hollow feeling probably had to do with the knowledge that during one of the most connected series of moments I'd ever had with another human being, there had been a stain, a dark shadow on the proceedings. An act of mine, which, if known, would've precluded the whole thing, caused it to all come crashing down. The stain somehow negated the rich satisfying experience, rendered its foundation false, transformed the experience into a charade.

In the movie *The Pope of Greenwich Village*, there are two guys—cousins, I think—who grew up together as tough street kids in what was then an Italian neighborhood in Greenwich Village. They're in their early thirties. And the more wild, screwed-up of the two, for the hundredth time, does something stupid, and gets them both fired from their well-paying jobs at an old school Italian restaurant. Later that night, they're standing on a sidewalk and arguing. The more grounded one gets frustrated trying to get the screwed-up one to face up to the fact that he's fucked up again. After a few minutes of getting nowhere, the grounded guy walks away in disgust.

The screwed-up one calls after him, "Hey, man. Let's go watch the sun come up, like the old days." Getting no response, he shouts, "Hey, *shaloot*, we'll sit and have a couple of cognacs like gentlemen."

The grounded guy stops, turns around and stands there for a few moments. Then he walks back to his cousin and says, "Hey, let me tell you something. I don't have time to watch the sun come up. *Capiche!* I don't have time!"

September 1994 to April 1995.

After Istanbul, Lucien and I had numerous good times together back in New York, that fall and winter, and into the spring. The day he got back, he made it official with Sharon that they were over. He maneuvered it so that she was the one who verbalized the decision. For a few days, she maintained the fiction it was her choice, until she couldn't hide the hurt.

Lucien and I hit the frontier-like Lower East Side in a big way—great bars like Bob's and 205. Lucien got into another expression from *Performance* for a couple of weeks: "I like to put the frighteners on flash little twerps like you."

My phrase at the time was "the ass-lick and the grovel." As in, "Lucien, you know about that, don't you? The ass-lick and the grovel?"

One night, we spied Peggy (aka Piggy) across the room at a party, and Lucien remarked drily, "Roll her around in flour and you still won't find the wet patch. Tell her to fart and give us a hint."

He and I were talking on the phone one day, and out of the blue he said, "What does the guy say? United we stand, divided we're…what? Bothered? No, that's not it."

"United we stand, divided we fall," I said.

"No, that's the standard expression. What I'm trying to remember is what one of the gangsters in *Performance* says. United we stand. Divided we're…buggered. No." It wouldn't come to him.

A few days later, in the middle of a conversation, he exclaimed, "Lumbered! United we stand. Divided we're lumbered."

Janey dumped me. Hard. It turned out, while I was in Istanbul, she was having serious gropes in various downtown nightspots with a young hipster named Andre, resulting in her being infatuated with the intensity of a teenager, thinking about him every moment, night and day, all that crap. She was only twenty-three, not that far removed from her teenage years. I learned about it all by reading her journal, which she'd conveniently left open on the coffee table in my apartment. See, there is some justice in the world. If anybody had it coming, it was me. In the course of the break-up, she got upset because I petulantly held onto a pair of boots I'd recently given her. I said to her, "Hey, shitty things happen to shitty people." I probably should have thought about that one a bit myself.

Just before our split, she told me that she and Sharon had an erotic session together in the hot tub out in Wainscott.

————————————

It may be that Lucien did have some complicity in what happened between Sharon and me, if only in the way he conducted his life. He was drawn to pushing the disturb button deep inside himself. The sensations he pursued encompassed unsettling ones as well as pleasing ones. He chose the twisted thrill of being with a sexy beautiful young woman who regularly went to the edge of betraying him and seemed like she might go over the line at any moment. He chose being with her though it included distinctly queasy feelings at times.

But no, he didn't want his friend to fuck his girlfriend. He was not that complicit.

He probably knew on some level that I was capable of betraying him. He was perceptive and knew me well. But he probably thought, as did I, it was irrelevant because Sharon would never have sex with me. He must have forgotten about the hell-hath-no-fury concept and the powerful drive of revenge. I'm profoundly sorry I didn't do better by him.

———————————————

"It's about the killing of a fascination." The Frenchies had a goddamn comment for everything. This time, though, I think the observation was off the mark. Certainly, when a fascination isn't reciprocated with at least a modicum of positive response, resentment can arise on the part of the intrigued person, maybe even a desire to erase the fascination, crush it. Maybe there was malice in my actions.

I believe, however, Lucien genuinely enjoyed our friendship. And I don't think it was a shortcoming in his affinity for me that prompted my stupidity. Besides, I enjoyed my fascination. It was far from unpleasant, hardly something I wanted to smash.

What happened was really about a staggeringly idiotic loss of a glorious friendship, one of rare quality. And for what? For sex? Ego? Because my character was weak and selfish, and I wasn't capable of conducting my life in accordance with what was truly important?

Or because I was on a never-ending quest for kicks and didn't know when to stop.

It was a deeply felt loss, and, as any imbecile should have known, the thrill wasn't remotely worth it. Not even close.

Fall 1994.

It came out that Lucien wasn't as nonchalant as he seemed regarding all of Sharon's transgressions. After they split, he told me about a time when the two of them had been in Miami with his uncle, a renowned theater director, and his uncle's boyfriend. They were all out at a club one night, and Sharon got up to her usual antics, but this time took it really far. I gather she basically humped some Cubano pretty boy on the dance floor, getting down and dirty. She always thought it was so cool that Lucien was confident enough to be chill about her behavior. It was almost as if they had an open relationship to the extent of heavy flirting. That night, if he'd been with friends who knew the score, he might well have maintained his studied indifference and let it slide, but this was his uncle. And his uncle said something to him about it, either out of concern or dismay. Lucien was stingingly embarrassed. I gather that for once he spoke quite angrily to her about her outrageousness.

Hey, even Scott the dental student went into the bathroom and threw up.

———————————

November 1994

After Lucien and Sharon split up, one of the Frenchies said to me that Sharon epitomized for me everything I hated about women. I think hate is too strong a word, but there probably was some truth in the remark. After all, almost everybody has at least a smidgeon, if not more, of negative feelings or perceptions about the opposite sex, whether they'll admit it or not. The question is how strong those feelings or perceptions are, and whether the person recognizes they are generalizations that have exceptions and should be policed. Yes, I probably have a mild dislike for women in general. Someone like me has inevitably had his share of bad experiences with women, some deserved, some not. Whatever level of negativity I have toward women, Sharon definitely brought out the worst of it in me.

If anything, I think it's more likely I suffer from misanthropy than misogyny.

When I was in college, a sophomore I think (being sophomoric has always been a strong suit of mine, as abundantly illustrated herein), I bought a book based on the title alone. I was in the college bookstore getting my assigned texts for the fall semester, and the title of the book on the shelf grabbed and held my eighteen-year-old attention. *Someday All My Friends Are Going to Be Strangers* by Larry McMurtry. At the time, I'd never heard of him or the book. It was one of his early novels.

Despite my youth, I intuitively knew there was truth in the strange extreme statement. (Like when you first hear the classic book title *You Can Never Go Home Again*, and you're too young to understand what it means, but you sense the words are profound. You can feel it.) So I bought the McMurtry book, and it was excellent.

Over the ensuing years, my youthful intuition proved correct. As people, we very much want to believe that our choices of friends and lovers are based mostly on feelings of liking and loving, on mutual enjoyment of one another. But the truth is our relationships are very much a product of circumstances, more so than most of us ever want to admit. And circumstances usually change and sometimes go away entirely. Things like people being in the same place or situation, or being lonely or not lonely at a particular time, or enjoying the same things. Conditions like that play an enormous role in who our friends and lovers are at any one point in time. And when the conditions shift or disappear, it's a real eye-opener to see how relationships can transform or fade, even fall by the wayside.

There are people you think for sure you're going to know forever, close friends, soul-mates, kindred spirits. And what happens? You grow in different directions, or one grows and the other doesn't. Geography intervenes. Or you have a massive falling-out and never really get past it. Or the strains of life, the tricky dynamics of relationships, getting older, all slowly muddy the waters without you ever really knowing exactly what happened.

As the years go by, you find that a sizeable number of people you've been close to are essentially gone from your life, and you don't always even know precisely how it happened, or why.

I, of course, didn't have to lose Lucien, at least not when I did. All I had to do was not fuck his girlfriend. And who knows, maybe then we would have been friends for years to come. Maybe for life.

Trent Reznor (and later Johnny Cash) sang poignantly, "Everybody I know goes away in the end."

Or as I say, "People come, people go. It's called life."

_____

April 1995.

Have you ever sat by yourself in the afternoon just thinking? Feeling? Maybe on a couch in your living room. And as the daylight gradually fades and turns to dusk, your eyes adjust and you don't even notice the room get dark. You don't get up to turn on the light. Until there comes a point when you realize you're just sitting there in the dark.

That's what happened to me after I got off my last phone call with Lucien.

I had called him, all jovial. "Hey, man. How're you doing?"

"Okay."

His voice sounded strange, distant. "Whatta you been up to?"

"Hm, I ran into Sharon last night at 205."

"What was that like?"

"Interesting. I learned a few things."

I froze at my end of the line. "Like what?"

"David," he said, tiredness in his voice. "How could you be so fucking stupid?"

I was silent for several moments. "Man, I'm sorry. It was really dumb. Colossally dumb. What can I say? I'm really sorry."

We hung up shortly after that. His tone of voice and manner conveyed It was a stone-cold given that getting past it was not going to be a possibility.

The last I heard of Sharon, she'd taken to calling herself Virginia and was living with a banker boyfriend, who'd bought her thirty thousand dollars worth of clothes in a spree on their second date. She was living with him, and he was bankrolling her new hobby of collecting art.

"That's a scary thought," said Matthew.

What can I say? Lucien helped me feel more alive than I've ever felt before or since. For me, he was Withnail, Lord Henry, and Shamus, all rolled into one. As good as it gets. An enchanter. How many times in your life are you going to have a friend like that? A spirited life-giving character with humor and charm? For me, Lucien was the stuff of living life to the full.

I guess the time had come for me to find that inside myself.

As he used to say with his wry grin, "It's a funny old world."

ACKNOWLEDGMENTS

In *Lucien And I*, I refer to, and in some cases quote from, many other novels, a screenplay, a play, and a number of songs. This is inherent in the collage-like nature of *Lucien And I*. Every reference is reverential, and I have the utmost respect for the artworks and artists concerned. The numerous artists and artworks are: Iain Banks (*The Wasp Factory*), Pat Barker (*Regeneration*), Saul Bellow (*The Adventures of Augie March*), Paul Bowles (*The Sheltering Sky*), William Boyd (*The New Confessions*), Frank Black (the song *Hey*), Donald Cammell (*Performance*), Lloyd Cole (the song *Rattlesnakes*), Bob Dylan (the songs *Sad-eyed Lady of the Lowlands* and *It's Alright, Ma*), Federico Fellini with Ennio Flaiano and Tullio Pinelli (*La Dolce Vita*), William Friedkin (*The Boys* in the Band), Christopher Hampton (*Les Liaisons Dangereuses*), Stanley Kubrick (*A Clockwork Orange*), John Le Carre (*The Naïve and Sentimental Lover*), Andrew Marvell (*To His Coy Mistress*), Michael McDermott (the song *The Idler, The Prophet, And A Girl Called Rain*), Larry McMurtry (*Someday All My Friends Are Going to Be Strangers*), John Milius with Francis Ford Coppola (*Bladerunner*), Vincent Patrick (*The Pope of Greenwich Village*), Trent Reznor (the song *Hurt*), Bruce Robinson (*Withnail And I*), Mike Scott (the song *The Pan Within*), Mark E. Smith (his rants), Paul Westerberg (the song *Black-eyed Susan*), Oscar Wilde (*The Picture of Dorian Gray*), and Jeannette Winterson (*The Passion*). I thank profoundly each and every one of these talented artists.

For their help and support, I would like to thank Joel Hochman, Olga Vladi, Jessica Gorham, Julie Mosow, Martha Hughes, Lorraine Fico-White, Sylvia Coleman, Gae Buckley, Rez Safinia, Dean Wareham, Kimball Higgs, Lucy Kaylin, Don Kelly, Joe Jablonski, and Duncan Bird.

I would also like give a very special thank-you to Dana, Toby and Billie for all their love and support.

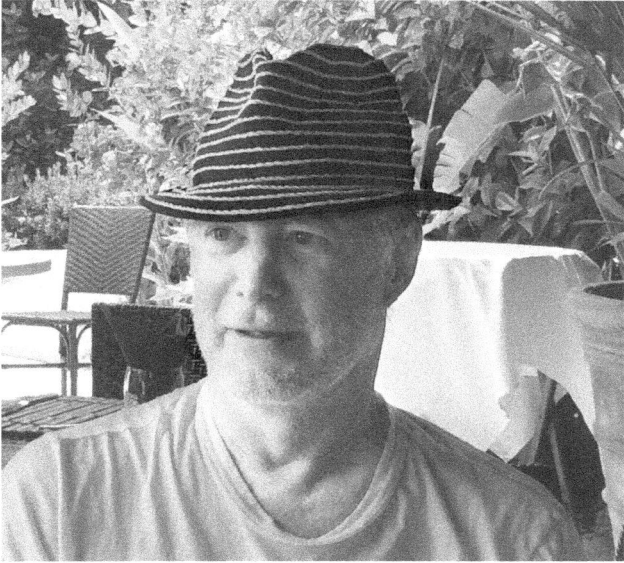

About the Author

Danny Wynn is a novelist whose first published work of fiction was a novella called *Man from the Sky*, set in Majorca, which is currently being made into a motion picture. Before that, he was an executive in the music industry and part-time fiction writer. He has lived and worked in New York City, London and Los Angeles, and now resides in the West Village with his wife and two children.

www.ingramcontent.com/pod-product-compliance
Lightning Source LLC
Chambersburg PA
CBHW030107070426
42448CB00036B/316